GREENWICH VILLAGE VIGNETTES

To STU + LIV

Love Dennis
(Shark)

GREENWICH VILLAGE VIGNETTES

How sweet it was
when the Village was
mine!
        Best wishes,
        Butch

ALFRED CANECCHIA

*Cover art by MaryAnn Hughes-Leake, formerly of Hampton, now living in
Carrollton, Virginia*

To order additional copies of this book, contact:
Xlibris Corporation
1-888-795-4274
www.Xlibris.com
Orders@Xlibris.com
26167

CONTENTS

Part One: In My Life

Part Two: Sex, Drugs & Rock-n-Roll

For my sons,
Aubrey and Arden

DEDICATION

To Anna Genovese Canecchia, who was both mother and father to me. She taught me how to live and how to die.

To Umberto Canecchia, my father's brother, and Marie Genovese Canecchia, my mother's sister, who were a second set of parents. Without them, my life would have been half what it was.

And to my sister, Carole, the first person in our family to attend and graduate college. She opened that door and I followed her through. It changed both our lives.

"I should have been a pair of ragged claws
Scuttling across the floors of silent seas."

The Love Song of J. Alfred Prufrock 1917
T.S. Eliot

Introduction

Greenwich Village Vignettes is a collection of short stories, or vignettes, chronicling a boy's coming of age during the time period after the Second World War, to the close of the tumultuous and life-changing decade of the 1960's.

The area was always known for its artists, bohemians and intellectuals. My world consisted of an Italian-American ghetto, with all the hopes, pitfalls and myriad characters such an environment produced.

Pictures emerge that are happy, sad, funny, poignant and tragic. Pictures of life that are an homage to the Greenwich Village I knew and grew up in, and to those who passed through there with me.

These recollections are based upon factual events. To a limited degree, sequences have been rearranged or juxtaposed to fit the story line. Ultimately, it is a memoir and not a document of history. Any failure to be exact is due to the many years that separate me from their occurrence. It is what I remember, and relying upon that, in itself, exposes its fallibility.

PART ONE
IN MY LIFE

Growing Up

The Village . . . . The Block

I was born and raised in a tenement on the Lower West Side of Manhattan, in Greenwich Village. The year was 1945. At that time, the area was mainly an Italian community with sprinklings of Irish, German, Polish, Portuguese, Puerto Rican and other immigrants. The majority was people of Southern Italian descent.

Technically, the Village ran from 14th Street on the north to Canal Street on the south. Its eastern and western borders ran from 5th Avenue to the Hudson River.

Italians, being very provincial, stayed near to home. Thus, it took years to explore this entire landscape. As a child, my universe was a square, shaped between 6th and 7th Avenues east to west, and 4th and Bedford Streets, north to south. Everything one could possibly need seemed to be contained in that small five to six block section. Our Lady of Pompeii Church and School, the produce-selling pushcarts on Bleecker Street, along with meat, fish, bread and pastry stores, fostered feelings of security and independence from the outside world. Living was isolated and self-sufficient. The Italians liked it that way.

Another thing Italians were fond of were nicknames. They were usually given out of fun, affection, or derision. Many colorful characters and personalities made them abundant and they served several purposes. These names were used to describe one's physical attributes, what one did for a living, or just an inexplicable labeling. Often, it was simply a way of distinguishing one person from another. Thus there was Tony the Bug, Tony Botts, or Anthony Bags. If you possessed a big nose you became Peetie

Pecker or Johnny Beak. Totally meaningless appellations, such as B-Bomb, Dit, Besh, and Geesh, were common.[1]

Two boys who worked at their parent's stands at Saint Anthony's Feast shucking clams and selling sausage and pepper sandwiches were called Jo-Jo Clams and Vinny Sauseech. This custom ran the gamut, from Tiny, Shorty and Skinny, to Fatman, Brother Fat and Fat Anna.

This practice did not escape the imagination, or lack of it, in my family. To begin with, my mother Anna was a woman who stood less than five feet tall. She was dubbed Wee or Weetsie, due to her diminutive stature. I found it difficult to distinguish which situations called for the choice in salutation. I decided Wee was for formal occasions, used by those outside the family, and Weetsie was more intimate and affectionate, reserved for people who knew her well.

Regardless of how she was addressed, it was a mistake to take her height as a disability or sign of weakness. Through the hardships in her life, she developed tremendous inner strength and fortitude. Standing her ground, like a little Napoleon, she would refuse to back down from any situation. Threats, coercion and bully tactics were inconsequential. She'd stand tapping her tiny foot on the ground, glaring at her nemeses, whomever they may be. My sister and I learned at an early age not to cross her. We got the message and did what we were told. This attitude and stance convinced others not to challenge her. No one did.

My mother's Aunt Angie, my Great aunt, had mastered this nickname business. When her first male child was born she called him Sonny. A couple of years later, when she gave birth to another boy, she called him Brother. They were rarely referred to by their given names of Anthony and Ralph. I was named Alfred, after my father. As soon as I was brought home from the hospital, my Great aunt turned to my mother and said, "Weetsie, we're gonna get confused with two Alfreds in the house." She pointed to me and proclaimed, "He's Butch." And so it was.

---

[1]   See Appendix A.

Many blocks in the neighborhood were able to furnish the basic necessities for living. Having a grocery, candy store and laundry, as Jones Street had, provided some of the essentials. At the corner intersection of Bleecker stood John's Pizzeria, Trio Bread and Bakery, Al & Ann's Luncheonette, Mandaro's cheese and olives, Ottomanelli meats, Rothman's Clothing and the hardware store, all combined, furnished the rest.

The building I grew up in, 15 Jones Street, was located on a short block between Bleecker and West 4th Street, just south of 7th Avenue. It was a five-story walk up built at the turn of the century. We lived in small railroad apartments that might be described as cold water flats, except, we had hot water. The bathtub was in the kitchen. You had to leave the apartment to use the toilet, situated in the hallway.

Our apartment was on the fifth floor, front. I lived there from 1945 till the day I married, December 7th, 1968. It was blistering hot in the summer and cold and drafty in the winter. On frosty nights I dreaded going to the toilet. There were reasons, I believed, for my trepidation.

Being alone in the dark hall, my childhood imagination would take over. I'd conjure up visions of villains stealthily descending the dim staircase leading to the roof. Their purpose was to snatch me and carry me away. It was always a frantic exercise to get the key in the bathroom door, enter the room and lock myself in, before being kidnapped.

There were other disturbing aspects to tenement life. My building, like others, was infested with roaches. While lying in bed, awaiting sleep, they'd crawl across my face and body. Their variety amazed me. Black, brown, red and an occasional white, or "albino," would make an appearance. With the windows open in summertime, huge water bugs, or "clocks" as we called them, found their way up from the ground. They usually frequented the sewers. The ability to fly gave them an extra measure of fright and intimidation.

For a young child, fear, mystery and adventure, could all be found in the basement. I was always wary entering its dark confines. Once, after playing on the street, my sister Carole and I were taken there to shower off the dirt and grime. She inadvertently backed up against the boiler and severely burned the flesh on her behind. That was the last time I remember her going down to the basement.

From time to time, as I grew older, I had cause to go down to check a fuse or defective circuit breaker. I found it hard to shake that eerie feeling. The stories I was told didn't help.

My maternal grandfather, who was a stepfather to my mother, was one of several male family members I would never know. My mother's biological father, Leon, died in her childhood. Exactly how, and under what circumstances, was never revealed. His life was totally hidden, and because of her young age at the time of his passing, it may have been as much a mystery to her as it was to us. Pictures of him or stories about him never surfaced during her life. It was one of several topics she never brought up. After her death, in the mid-1990's, tales emerged indicating Leon may have died in prison. Other uncorroborated gossip suggests he was the brother of Vito Genovese. This is pure speculation and the surname is far too common to assume any connection. Like my father, and his father, most of the immediate male figures in my reach would die before my time.

I often was reminded of my step-grandfather's habit of taking a gallon of *Chianti* down to the basement and sitting in a chair in the dark. He would patiently wait, drinking his wine, until a rat came upon him. Catching the rodent with his bare hands, he would snap its neck.

This was not done for pest control. It was a bizarre form of amusement, which became one of his favorite pastimes. What an imaginative way to seek entertainment. His drink and his diversion kept him content. Born Louis Boitano, everyone called him by his nickname, Happy.

Happy had other curious customs. When invited to dinner he'd bring his own knife and fork. He also carried a pistol that he placed on the table next to his plate. I can picture his anxious hosts frantically preparing a meal they hoped would be to his satisfaction.

My sister and I got along well for siblings of opposite sex, living in such close quarters. Two exceptions come to mind. Once she threw me down a flight of stairs for verbally abusing her. She was overweight as a child and my favorite, taunting nickname for her was Fatman. I paid her back sometime later by throwing a fork across the table that just missed her head. Whenever I did something naughty and stupid, I'd crawl under the kitchen table where my mother had difficulty reaching me. There, crouched in a corner, I'd momentarily escape the wrath of Weetsie. Depending on the severity of the infraction, I was allowed to stay put until things cooled down, or be forcibly extricated for a walloping.

Our cousin, Lillian Lamarsch, lived down the hall in the rear apartment diagonally across from us. Her mother, Frances, was our mother's aunt. The line they lived in was the only one in the building having the toilet inside. Because of this feature, there was less room for Fran, Lillian and her father Larry to share. Having more space, Lillie would visit us. She was four months younger than my sister, providing a perfect playmate.

Our early play sessions revolved around the ubiquitous pee pot. This device was a fixture until I became toilet trained. Kicking this receptacle around as we moved about dramatizing our imaginative fantasies, became routine. Simple scenarios, such as Lolly, Lolly and the Baby, where I was a defenseless child attended to by a pair of loving siblings, became a vehicle for them to torture me. When things got out of hand, the girls always stuck together while placing the blame on me. Lolly and Lolly laughed their heads off, while the Baby scurried under the table. This was a typical situation in which the name-calling and verbal menacing began. It would start simply, and rapidly accelerate, becoming more bellicose and ominous in nature and tone. My mother's mantra followed a pattern: "Don't start in with me. Don't start in with me, you son of a bitch. Don't start in with me, you son of a bitch, bastard." After warming up, the physical threats followed. "Keep it up. Keep it up and I'll crack you. Keep it up and I'll crack your face. Keep it up and I'll crack your face wide open." Aside from the rare beatings we received, which consisted of a few smacks, as we grew older my sister and I realized Weetsie's bluster and bravado was essentially a facade.

In time our games became more sophisticated. The girls evolved into beautiful, helpless czarinas, subjugated to my scheming alter ego, the evil and sinister Borgevitch. The tables had turned. I was chasing them around, and implicating them as the villains in all the mishaps.

My Great, great Uncle Mike Marone, and his brother Ralph, my Great grandfather, owned the building for a period of time. Before I was born, my father and his brother had an opportunity to buy the place for $10,000.00. Such an amount constituted a life's savings for two truck drivers and was out of reach, but would have been a prudent investment if attainable.

Today, the property is worth millions, especially after the renovations due to the fire in 1973. Duplex apartments, some with fireplaces, replaced the linear design with the bathroom in the kitchen and the toilet in the hall. This renewal glamorized the block and initiated the gentrification process in this part of the Village.[2] The block received notoriety when it was pictured on the cover of the 1963 album, "The Freewheelin' Bob Dylan."

My cousin Kathy, who was born in 1951 and raised in 11 Jones Street, lived there until the fire. In 1973 she moved to Leroy Street with her mother Velia and her sister Jacki. They obtained, along with her Aunt Louise and her daughter Theresa, a ten-year lease in a brownstone building that was owned by Pompeii Church.

My father's sister, Louise Canecchia Callahan, had strong ties to the church. She worked all her life for Edward and Theresa O'Toole. They owned a store on Church Street that sold a variety of religious articles, statues, rosaries, books and other products associated with Catholicism. This venture made them wealthy and their subsequent charitable contributions culminated in having a building in their name erected at St. Vincent's Hospital. Through her association with the O'Tooles, and because of her older sister Yolanda's vocation as a nun, Louise was in good standing with the clergy.

From her employers she gained a certain savoir-faire. Under their guidance and counsel, she saved and invested her money

---

[2]   See Appendix B.

wisely. Her lease on a house owned by the church was due, in large part, to these connections.

Such influences, apparently, had no bearing after her demise. Her nieces, along with her daughter, were not offered new terms at the expiration of the original contract, even though Louise had used a considerable amount of her own funds in modernizing the place. Had she lived, she would have been in a good position to offer to buy the building or continue leasing on a long-term basis.

A year after moving in, April 1974, Velia died. The next year, August 1975, Louise passed away. At forty-seven and fifty years of age, both, by modern standards, were young women. These unforeseeable events left Kathy and Jacki, ages twenty-four and twenty three, alone and responsible for their teenage cousin.

After working and putting herself through night college, Kathy secured a job at Saint Vincent's Hospital as an administrator and later attended their nursing school. In 1983 she went to a local realtor to seek an apartment in the neighborhood. Ironically, the agent showed her an apartment in 11 Jones Street, the building she had lived in for twenty-two years. Eleven Jones had escaped the destructive damage of the fire and was basically intact. No major renovations were apparent, and the bathtub was still in the kitchen. When shown her old apartment, on a different floor, my cousin was slightly amused. When told the rent was $850.00, her amusement turned to laughter. The last rent she remembered her mother paying ten years earlier was $42.00 a month. The apartment may have been worth the asking price. However, she could not bring herself to pay such an amount, not at that address.

Her lease ended and she would have to leave a colorful block filled with childhood memories and special attractions. One was the vendor who sold pretzels, chestnuts and knishes to children on the street and those waiting to enter Pompeii School. He was a tall, lean, funny looking man with a big nose. A large Adam's apple protruded through the skin in his neck, giving the appearance he had swallowed a golf ball. In the cold weather he wore a cap with earflaps to keep him warm. He had a strange affliction. His hands and body shook in an uncontrollable manner. As the students became aware of his disability, knishes suddenly rose in popularity. Each order was accompanied by the refrain, "with extra salt, please." The vendor would hold the knish up in one hand while trying to apply salt from a shaker in the other. Due to his condition most of the salt missed its mark, landing on the ground. Too young to realize this man had a serious illness, his gyrations and futile attempts to deliver the food as requested delighted us.

Another fun thing to do on Leroy Street was to go to "I Don't Know's." This was a delicatessen selling farm eggs, fresh mozzarella, ricotta and other Italian products. When my mother could afford such a luxury, her usual habit was to patronize Mandaro's cheese store. The aroma of the multitude of cheeses that wafted through the store was a catalyst to one's appetite. Mandaro also carried a variety of pickles and olives. As a small boy I remember the barrels that held these products being as tall as I was. They lined the sawdust filled floor in front of the counter displaying the *latticini freschi*. These casks brimmed with green, black and brown olives, or whole pickles that floated in thick brine.

On the way to the store I often encountered an older fellow who had severe learning disabilities. Most thought he was retarded and everyone called him Crazy Carlo. His daily routine was to run errands for the merchants on Bleecker Street. Due to his handicaps, he took heavy abuse from his peers. Whenever we younger kids tried to interact with him his anger and frustration poured out. His response to any attempted dialogue was terse and unwavering. No matter what was said to him, he replied, "Detatta-ere, you futtin-ardon." Since this reaction became predictable, we often spoke to him in order to elicit this response. His delivery, in a Dead End Kids cadence, was laughable.

As I grew older and could travel farther on errands, my mother had options other than Mandaro's corner cheese store. Occasionally, she'd say, "Go to I Don't Know's and get me a pound of pot cheese." When I asked what pot cheese was, she snapped, "Just get me some reegott."

The first time I went there, I had no idea what she was referring to. Entering the store I said, "Good morning," to the proprietor, who responded, "I don't know." I said, "I'd like a pound of pot cheese." He replied, "I don't know." After this exchange he disappeared into a back room and returned with a small package wrapped in wax paper. I asked "How much?" He answered, "I don't know."

We were at an impasse. I thought to myself, he's running the place. If he doesn't know, how am I to know? I asked again, "How much is it, please?"

He remained silent, for a moment or two, as if the question baffled him, then blurted out, "One dolla a fifty cent," and immediately followed his declaration with, "I don't know." Amid the disorder and indecision, you'd end up leaving with what you came in for. How that was accomplished, I don't know.

My cousin Kathy would leave the Village to live in Brooklyn. She is still a nurse at Saint Vincent's. Her job, if not her domicile, keeps her in touch with her roots. Once you've lived in Greenwich Village it is always a part of you.

Early Troubles

I wasn't a sickly child, yet several incidents occurred putting me on a path of medical mishaps. My family physician did not believe in circumcision. To this day I have mixed feelings about this. The doctor's instructions were to clean my penis by pulling back the foreskin. While bathing me, my mother would routinely follow these orders to clear out any foreign material or bacteria that may have lodged there. The water, with gentle patting, was sufficient to do the job. This process worked well until something went wrong. During one of these baths the handling of my "little dew-drop," as my mother's sister Marie referred to it, caused blood to engorge the head of my penis, after the skin had been pulled back. This resembled a blown up balloon that was twisted in the middle, leaving air at both ends of the pinch. The foreskin could not move forward until the blood ran back from the head. The blood could not flow back from the head without the foreskin moving forward, releasing the pinch. It was a catch-22.

Being poor didn't afford me either immediate or quality attention for situations that arose. In dire need of medical care, I was instead brought to a place of business. In what appeared to be a photography studio, I was administered to by the proprietor and his wife, who were both friends of my mother. This did nothing to improve my plight. Lying exposed on a table, left me open to embarrassment, ridicule and humiliation. Other adults were summoned to examine and comment upon my predicament. Discomfort aside, total strangers were getting more than a passing glance at my "little dew-drop," which at this point, was as big as it could get.

Flabbergasted, and unable to alleviate the pain, my mother belatedly took me to the emergency room at Saint Vincent's Hospital. There, they proceeded to put ice packs around the inflamed area. Eventually, the swelling reduced, releasing the foreskin and returning my penis to normal.

This proved to have a lasting effect on my psyche. Years later, during sexual encounters with virgins, or any woman who was vaginally tight, I'd anticipate my foreskin being pulled back during intercourse and getting stuck in that position again. Visions of being rushed off to the hospital for ice pack treatments filled my mind. For a time, my sexual adventurousness was stunted. As I grew into my late teens, hormonal drives and natural desires enabled me to overcome any lingering anxieties.

The next trouble came when I was in the fifth grade. My cousin Yolanda was my classmate. The school had two classes for each grade. Some years we ended up together in the same class. She was a month older and more socially and sexually aware. Her interest in the opposite sex blossomed long before mine did.

We would often visit together at her apartment in 11 Jones. One of our favorite treats was a concoction made by her mother, my Aunt Eleanor. Aunt El would separate the whites from the egg yolks and beat them by hand. No one yet had an electric mixer. Her process was to whip the eggs into a creamy froth. The addition of just the right amount of sugar and milk resulted in a delicious dessert. It was her version of a *zabaglione* without the Marsala wine. When our mothers were distracted Yolanda seized every opportunity to practice her kissing techniques on me. While growing up, we were truly kissing cousins.

I had a weak eye muscle causing my eye to drift to the side. Tiredness, due to lack of sleep, excess reading or watching television brought this about. To exacerbate the condition, a fight in school prompted a classmate to stab me in the corner of the eye with a pencil. My cousin Yolanda screamed at the top of her lungs while blood trickled down my face.

I was scheduled for surgery at Manhattan Eye Ear Nose and Throat Hospital to correct this infirmity. My uncle, my father's brother, Umberto, accompanied my mother and me. After my father's death, he and his wife Marie were a second set of parents to my sister and I. This was a natural evolution of two sisters marrying two brothers. The children of these unions are first cousins, but growing up we were as close as brothers and sisters.

My uncle was called "The Professor." He was a short man who stood approximately five feet six inches tall. He had a twinkle in his hazel eyes, and the color often changed from green to gray, depending on the reflection of light from the shade of the clothes he wore. Both he and his mother displayed a peculiar nasal feature. At the tip of their nose, which was an ample Italian proboscis, one could see a round shaped skin blemish. Grandma displayed a blue dot, while my uncle's was red. They were the only two people in the family with this distinction.

My uncle's parents both emigrated from Italy through Ellis Island. They had eight children. Six survived to adulthood. A daughter, my Aunt Yolanda, joined a convent. She entered the Missionary Sisters of the Sacred Heart at sixteen, and died there of pneumonia at the age of twenty. My cousin, my classmate during this incident, was named after her.

My grandmother previously lost two children. One at birth, and another who survived several years. Nineteen forty-six was an exceptionally bad year for her. She lost her son, my father, aged thirty, on May 2nd, and her husband, aged fifty-eight, on May 27th. I was fifteen months old and have no memories of either. I was told my grandfather was a chef in several noted restaurants uptown. He eventually opened a place of his own in the Village in the early 1930's.

Although he had a large family, which was common at the time, he did well enough to send my uncle for violin lessons. His peers picked up on his avocation and began calling him Professor. The name stuck well beyond his musical studies. His real name Umberto was Italian for Humbert. At his job as a truck driver they called him Albert, or Al. As time passed, Professor, was shortened to Pro. All his life, I referred to him as Uncle Pro.

The minor details of this particular hospital stay are vague. The highlights are burnished in my memory. Immediately prior to the operation, I was strapped onto a table while a handful of doctors and nurses huddled around me. Without warning or verbal preparation, a mask was held over my face, exuding a noxious, sickening smell. I became nauseous and dizzy, with the first inhalation of the gas emanating from this device. Violently tossing my head back and forth, I struggled to escape the vapors' power and inevitable control. I lost the battle, reluctantly surrendering my consciousness. I later learned they were administering ether. To this day, if I smell anything remotely resembling that odor, I am brought back to that moment and my stomach becomes queasy.

I slowly returned to the world. It was like awakening from a dream. My eyes opened to be met with darkness. Why was it so dark? I thought. I was groggy and disoriented. It took awhile to figure out where I was and what had happened. Bandages covered my eyes, keeping the light in the room to a glimmer. When I tried to move, I realized my arms were tied to the bed rails. A strap across my legs further limited my mobility. I knew what it felt to be alone in the universe.

Time was suspended, distorting the concept of how long I spent there. One afternoon my Uncle Pro came to visit me. He said I was being released the following day and promised to pick me up in his truck. The next day turned out to be the longest day of anxiety and anticipation in my life, and perhaps, the most disappointing. Every time a truck honked its horn on the street, I was certain it was my uncle coming to take me home. Believing any moment he'd appear, and being let down over and over, was emotionally exhausting and psychologically punishing. Long after dark I fell asleep, completely spent. My hopes had been shattered and I felt totally abandoned.

Years later I realized some bureaucratic error or change in my condition delayed my departure. However, on that day, I learned a good lesson. I learned what my mother learned years before. One had to be strong. One had to be patient. One had to wait and endure.

My paternal grandmother, Josephine Schettini Canecchia, lived at 243 Bleecker Street, across from Pompeii Church and School. Born in Italy in 1889, she came to America and was married in 1911. She lived at several addresses in the Village, raising her six children who survived to adulthood. This three-story walk-up is where I remember her living. She occupied a two-bedroom apartment on the top floor. It featured a large eat-in kitchen and a huge living room, accommodating a table to seat the whole family at dinner. Caesar's Pastry Shop was the storefront at the entrance of the building. Today it is called Rocco's. Next door was another *pasticceria* named Della Rova. It is now known as the Bleecker Street Pastry Shop.

My uncle would visit his mother as often as possible. Since many of his truck stops were in lower Manhattan, he'd park on Bleecker and make a lunch time visit. Stopping at Bosco's pork store for a cooked salami sandwich was his routine.

When time allowed, he'd stop by to say hello to Wee, and check on how we kids were doing. Once he presented me with the conundrum of choosing to live with him and his family or remain in the city with my mother. This was equivalent to asking a child to choose between his parents. It may have been disingenuous on his part, but it presented me with an agonizing decision. Grown-ups sometimes forget the power and impact their actions and words have upon the mind of a youngster.

Weetsie stood by anxiously awaiting my answer. She knew this was not a serious proposition and I was not going anywhere. Her fear lay in whether I would embrace such an offer. In doing so, I would present her with another abandonment, not physical, but emotional. I did the right thing in opting to stay with her and my sister. This was a game for the adults yet heart wrenching for me.

Another call proved to be very timely. Carole and I were sitting at the kitchen table, eating fruit and playing around, as children do. Suddenly, a large peach pit stuck in my throat. I couldn't breathe, turning blue in the face. My mother and sister panicked and were rendered useless. Providence took a hand. At that moment, a knock on the door revealed that Uncle Pro was on the other side. He rushed in, immediately taking charge of the situation. Picking me up, and turning me upside down, he pounded on my back until the pit shot out of my mouth. I was teary eyed and shaken up. My throat was sore and scratchy for days, but I was alive and breathing again.

We were fortunate to have him appear when he did. His concern about our welfare was genuine, making his visits more than welcome. I sensed, on that day, and other times during my life, my father was looking down and watching over us. My uncle often told me I was cheated by not having the opportunity to know my dad.

Soon after my first birthday, my father suffered a stroke and was placed in intensive care. As he lay in his hospital bed, Pro promised his brother he'd take care of us, if needed. My father died of asphyxiation, choking on his own vomit. My uncle and aunt kept that promise and could do no more than they did in acting as surrogates, in helping my mother to raise her children. We were always invited to their home to sleep over or celebrate special occasions. Often, we were included for summer vacations, and looked forward to them as a chance to escape the stifling heat of the city.

My uncle's boss, who owned the trucking company he drove for, employed a salesman named Frank. He was a pompous sort, always acting like a know it all. Because of his condescending nature we mockingly called "The Senator." He had a house on Lake Brantingham and sometimes offered the place to my uncle for a week or two during the summer. His payment usually involved handiwork of some kind, involving painting or minor repair work.

The Professor took care of the maintenance and cooked for the Senator who enjoyed a good Italian meal.

His favorite entrée was a chicken *cacciatore* in white scauce that Pro had perfected after learning the basic recipe from his father.

The most memorable times were spent over the Christmas and New Year holidays. When visiting during the year, we'd take public transportation, arriving by subway to the outer borough of Queens. Depending on the fluidity of finances, we'd take the bus, or walk the mile distance from Main Street to Mulberry Court.

On Christmas Eve two special things happened. First, my uncle, aunt and their two children, Joan and Joseph, picked us up in their car for the ride back to Flushing. Second, we always drove up 5th Avenue. The boulevard ran north in those days. Viewing the window displays of stores like Lord and Taylor, heightened our enthusiasm, which culminated in seeing the tree in Rockefeller Center. It was a thrill for us all. During the ride we sang our favorite carols. These are among the happiest recollections of my childhood.

Spending Christmas Eve with my cousins, Joan and Joseph, was a child's delight. My Uncle Pro always trimmed the tree to perfection. He took hours fussing with the decorations while strategically placing each bulb and ornament. Once the bubble lights warmed up they would effervesce in pointed tubes of red and green. Jo-Jo's Lionel electric train set careened around the track, circling the tree. The locomotive, the Pennsylvania Express, whistled and blew puffs of white smoke as it chugged along.

Uncle Pro and Aunt Marie's house was an attached townhouse with two levels and a basement. An outside patio, garage and adjacent yard, completed the property. A wonderful meal was always prepared during these holiday visits. The first course was a simple pasta with gravy, which was Jo-Jo's favorite. This was followed by either a chicken dish, roast pork or roast beef. Potatoes, escarole, spinach or string beans were served as vegetables. The salad came last, and I always complimented my aunt on how good it was. She found this hilarious. After consuming a meal of such abundance, my only commentary concerned the lettuce.

Devouring such a sumptuous meal I sometimes forgot my table etiquette and slurped and chewed while engaging in conversation. My relatives reprimanded me by saying, Hey, you're eating like a real Kowalski."

The only person I knew with that name was a wrestler of the period, Killer Kowalski. I made an effort to be more mannered. Each time I regressed they called me Kowalski.

The named intrigued me. I tried to figure out who it could be. Being a gourmand, The Senator came to mind. Not knowing his full name kept me from a positive identification.

As an adult, while watching "A Streetcar Named Desire," I came to the conclusion that Marlon Brando's portrayal of Stanley Kowalski, was the person they were comparing me to.

To keep Jo-Jo and myself out of trouble on these extended visits, Aunt Marie would give out chores to occupy us. Jo-Jo was given the job of cleaning the living and dining rooms. What this entailed was a light dusting of the furniture and vacuuming of the carpet. My aunt would emplore him to put some elbow grease into his effort and not perform like a girl. She compared him to a fictional chamber maid and would direct and warn him with the expression, "Now, don't do Katarina!"

From the time I was a child, I liked to see things done over or made to look like new. This was my way of reshaping the world into a better place. When my aunt gave me the task of polishing the silverware, I approached it with earnestness. She was amazed at the patience and attention I gave to this simple act, and always recognized my efforts by telling me how shiny and clean the table service looked. Aside from doing a good job, when she realized how much I enjoyed doing it, she brought forward all her gravy bowls, serving platters and candelabra. In the future, it became my responsibility to polish all the silver in the house.

Compared to my domicile, their home and lifestyle was middle class, but not nearly as impressive as my Great great Uncle Mike Marone's house on Oak Avenue. He lived a few blocks from my cousins and the entire family often gathered there for holiday celebrations. The house was built in the 1930's and was for some time the only structure on the block. The property had an extra lot that was used as a lawn for family gatherings and as an area for the children to romp and play. Until the end of the 1960's, the house remained the only one in the locality to still have additional land. It was a magnificent brick English Tudor that featured arched wooden doors, stained-glass windows and beamed ceilings.

The Marone lineage was enate. I never knew Bella, my maternal grandmother. She died of tuberculosis when my mother was a teenager. The same way my mother omitted her father from our lives, in like manner she never spoke about her mother or displayed any photographs. Maybe this was her way of dealing with the feelings of grief and abandonment.

Bella had four sisters that were my great aunts. Aunt Angie and Aunt Frances, the middle sisters, lived in 15 Jones Street. The oldest, Mamie, and her husband Eddie along with the youngest, Lillian, and her husband Joe Gaffney lived with Great great Uncle Mike on Oak Avenue.

My great aunts, in keeping with the code of silence, never spoke to me about Bella. I was often in their company, especially the two that lived in my building. They never took the opportunity to tell me about her. I found it curious no one offered me a picture saying, "This was your grandmother, my sister." On the other hand, I did not ask, nor was I expectantly waiting to be told. It just never happened. I still believe the responsibility for taking the initiative lied with the adults.

The sisters were all married and their spouses would provide entertainment and hilarity at these get-togethers which were held in the large basement room. Mamie's husband, Eddie Pritzlaff, was a character. He drank excessively and was prone to engage in pranks and buffoonery.

The dining table, under normal conditions, could seat about 14 people. Leafs were available to increase its capacity to twenty or more. The stately oak table had legs carved into lion's heads. It featured a buzzer button that in another setting would be used to summon servants. Invariably, someone would press the signal and Uncle Eddie would appear with a kerchief on his head, and a napkin folded over his arm, with the response, "You rang?" Over time, the ladies had the bell disconnected.

Another of his favorite antics was to lie in the middle of the floor with flowers across his chest. This attempt at mimicking a dead person laid out in a funeral parlor never went over well with the women. The men, having consumed their usual amount of boilermakers, found it enchanting.

Uncles Pete, Larry, Eddie and Joe, were all heavy drinkers. Uncle Pro could keep up with them all. Great great Uncle Mike, who lived into his nineties, smoked an occasional cigar, and drank therapeutic amounts of wine. Compared to the rest, his indulgences were Spartan. All the other adults, with a few exceptions, smoked, drank and ate with hearty appetites.

There was always plenty of potato chips and soda for the kids. Cases of White Rock, with all the various flavors: Cola, Grape, Orange, Lemon-Lime, Cherry, Cream, Vanilla Cream, Ginger Ale, Root Beer and Sasparilla, were in abundance.

To Lillian, Carole and I, the way our more fortunate cousins in Flushing lived was an eye opener. For three poor children growing up in a city tenement, this was a palace in a fantasy land. It presented a style of living that was something to aspire to.

On one evening during the holiday, the grown-ups wanted to be alone. They hoped to enjoy each others company without the interference of the children. Joseph and I stayed at his house while my sister Carole and cousin Lillian were left across the street. Our older cousins, Jean and Billy, lived their in a house that they owned. The adults all congregated at Oak Avenue to party and make merry.

Cousin Joseph soon tired of the available games and the capacity of our imaginations to keep us amused. He decided we would visit the girls across the way. It was dark and he planned to sneak over and surprise them. In itself, the visit would have been inconsequential. Jo-Jo made it much more intriguing when he chose to put a nylon stocking over his head while shining a flashlight under his chin. In this macabre outfit, he stood with his face pressed against the window of the front door, knocking and peering through the glass. When the girls came to answer the door, Lillian went berserk, screaming in an hysterical manner. She pulled herself together enough to place a call to Oak Avenue. Still in distress, she continued to yell into the phone incoherently.

The adults got into their cars and raced over to Mulberry Court to see what the matter was. Halfway through the girls' explanation, Uncle Pro recognized his son as the main engineer and culprit. On this occasion, as upon many others during Jo-Jo's free-spirited and somewhat rebellious youth, his father administered a thorough beating. Uncle Pro justified his actions by emphasizing how Joseph had "scared the daylights out of everybody."

This opportunity to demonstrate our maturity had been given against Weetsie's better judgment, and we were never left alone after that. It was at such times my mother would address my sister and me and deliver her hackneyed declaration, "We're never coming to Flushing again!"

Great great Uncle Mike was in a quandary as to whom to bequeath his property. He looked askance on his niece's husbands believing them to be either alcoholics, or womanizers. He settled upon the youngest, Lillian, thinking she would live the longest. Ironically, a few years after the house was put in her name, she died of cancer. Her husband Joe, a relative through marriage, became the owner. My Uncle Pro found this hard to accept. He felt the Marone heirs were cheated out of their share of this inheritance.

These concerns had no effect on me. I was happy to be with my cousins experiencing life in a fuller capacity. The quiet of the suburbs elicited sounds that delighted me. The melodic trill of birds warbling in the trees was in stark contrast to the banal coos of the pigeons we were familiar with. Late at night I could hear the whistle of a distant train passing through. In the morning, the engines of a plane flying to or from a nearby airport always sent me daydreaming. It reminded me of a boy who lived upstate that every couple of years would visit relatives on Jones Street. He had a gasoline powered model airplane that he guided by remote control. The noise it made echoed the sounds of the small single engine planes that sometimes flew over my cousins' home.

The one blemish attached to these visits was a condition of enuresis, which plagued me during my pre-pubic period. Whether any emotional, psychological or physiological factors had some influence, is debatable. The excitement of being with my cousins in the country, which to us, was anywhere outside the city, was enough. Whatever the cause, it happened invariably. When I slept over my cousins' I wet the bed. My doing this at home is unclear. Perhaps its occurrence, if so, in my own bed, was greeted without fanfare. In Flushing, a rubber mat was placed on the side of the bed where I slept with my cousin JoJo. Ostensibly, the pad protected the mattress from urine stains and odors. Each morning, upon awakening one of the adults would march up the stairs, enter the room and make an inspection. The words "He wet the bed again," was a refrain I'd hear over and over during those difficult years growing up.

Street Games and Football Weddings

There once existed a slew of street games, no longer in fashion, for kids growing up in the city. Ring-a-leevio, kick the can, hide and go seek, buck-buck, johnny on the pump, jump rope, boxball and skelsy.

Skelsy was a game that employed soda caps filled with melted wax from a candle. Once the wax hardened, weighing down the cap, it could easily be propelled with accuracy and direction, by a flick of the fingers. The playing area was chalk drawn on the street. The object was to be the first to land his cap on all the numbered boxes in sequential order. You gained an extra turn by hitting your opponent's cap while driving it further from its goal. Most games rested upon one's own imagination and ingenuity requiring little, if any, investment in hardware or equipment.

An oblong stick, clothespin, rubber band and nail, were all that were necessary to make a carpet gun. Discarded linoleum cut into small squares, served as ammunition.

Weetsie warned me immediately of its hazards. "This is not a toy, but a dangerous weapon that could blind someone."

I bombarded the buildings across the street, satisfying my desire to play with the contraption. My mother allowed this activity, hoping it would replace close range shootouts with my playmates.

Frustrated by her restraints on the carpet gun, I set my sights on pedestrians with a nother homemade projectile, the matchstick shooter. An empty spool of thread, matches and rubber band provided the necessary implements to launch an attack.

Aiming at the feet of passers-by, the matches ignited upon impact with the pavement. The victims of my ambushes searched upwards to locate the source of these exploding missiles. Nimbly drawing the shade kept me from being discovered.

There at the window, I counted cars and trucks in transit, viewed people in their daily routines and watched merchandise being loaded and unloaded into and out of the factories.

I spent many hours passing time observing the motions of the city.

One of the most complex enterprises was building a scooter. This undertaking was the exception to easy accessibility and low maintenance. The first thing that was required was a good pair of skates. Chicago roller skates were the preferred brand. This being the most expensive item in the project and the only one that had to be purchased. The other components were scrounged for. The search began for a two by four piece of lumber measuring about four feet in length. Once acquired, it served as a plank to which the skates were nailed at both ends. A wooden milk crate was attached atop this makeshift skateboard. Handles were added to the sides of the emerging vehicle for maneuverability. Bottle caps of all size and color adorned the front of the box. The scooter was ready for action! Chariot races commenced, filling our summers with a diversion both industrious and enjoyable.

As we grew older, stickball replaced kick-the-can and hide and go seek. All that was needed was a broomstick for a bat and a Spalding rubber ball. The game was usually played utilizing the length of the street. Set up like a baseball diamond, the ball was either pitched on a bounce, or thrown over-hand to a catcher. Another style was to play across the width of the street, using a building wall, with a strike zone marked out on its surface.

The most popular street game, and the one I was best at, was stoop-ball. The Greenwich House Pottery at 12 Jones Street, provided a convenient curb to hit the ball off. This game was also played across the width of the street. Bases were marked out in chalk with the foul lines arbitrarily set. The building directly across from the Pottery, was a three-story factory, located at 17 Jones. Occasionally, the ball was hit onto the roof of this structure, and considered a home run. The problem lay in retrieving the ball for further play. This was a dangerous reclamation that became a rite of passage for a boy growing up on my block.

The feat was to climb from my Great aunt Angie's bedroom window, up onto the factory roof. The first few times her son, my cousin Brother, demonstrated how this was accomplished. He was fourteen years older and already a man. I watched closely, knowing the time would come when I'd have to perform this stunt myself. When it did, I stood on the sill, barely able to reach the wall of the factory building across the way. Leaning forward, on stretched toes, I managed to grab hold and pull up onto the roof. I was guided and encouraged by the adults present, and the other kids who followed me into the apartment, to witness and to learn. One day, they would have their opportunity to prove themselves. I found the ball and quickly realized the hard part was still ahead. Getting back down proved to be the real trick. Lowering myself to the window ledge while facing backwards was enormously challenging. The notion that one slip meant a fall of three stories into the alley between the buildings, added to the risk. There are things done in the brashness of youth that ignore consequences. You did what had to be done. This was one of those things. I became very adept at this, and in time, a few of my peers learned to successfully navigate this act. We all shared in the thrill of it. After each retrieval, we'd leave the apartment and return to the street to continue our game.

On the other side of the factory, at 19 Jones, a strange couple routinely watched us play and after the game, held court. Louie the Lug, as he was called, and Ting-a-Ling, nee Theresa, were sidekicks. Something on the order of the Lone Ranger and Tonto. She being female made it more like a grotesque version of Roy Rogers and Dale Evans. They'd stand on the stoop and spin their tales. Actually, Louie would spin and Theresa would smoke and listen. I was curious about the nickname "The Lug." Was it a stupid fellow, or a nut to a bolt? You could have your pick. I didn't have the courage to question what Ting-a-Ling meant.

By any measure, Louie was disturbing. His hands hung limp at the wrist. Lifeless, glassy eyes, excreted yellow mucous that collected at the corners. Saliva dripped out of his mouth. At times it dangled on a long thin line, like silk thread from a spider's spinneret. He claimed to be a sheriff, with a horse that jumped from rooftop to rooftop. The tales grew more elaborate with each presentation. One horse with such abilities soon became a pack, with increased power to fly great distances. Sometimes he'd roll his eyes up into the back of his head, leaving only the whites showing. Though he was basically harmless, we were often frightened and repulsed by his continence. When asked for a rational explanation for his condition and behavior, the adults in my orbit offered no intelligent diagnosis. They simply said, "When he was a child, the ceiling fell on his head." I slept uneasily for quite a period of time, wondering if such a fate might befall me. As I matured, finding other places than my block to play and hang out, I gradually lost track of Louie and Theresa. Their absence was somehow as mysterious as their presence, leaving no idea what became of them.

Children of Italian descent were included in every social event and family gathering. Some of the best times took place at family weddings. The first such occasion I remember was my Aunt Rita's wedding in 1951. It took place at a Knights of Columbus auditorium in Queens. It was a modest affair. My older male cousins, Sonny and Brother, were serving in the armed forces during the Korean conflict, and were not present. As they returned home and married, their celebrations were held at formal catering halls.

Lennox Hall is the place I remember most of these events occurring. Located within walking distance from the neighborhood, on Houston Street and 2nd Avenue, this establishment furnished hall, food, drinks and band, at affordable prices. The so-called "football weddings," which were very popular in the 1950's, were held here. Cellophane wrapped sandwiches, piled high on trays, were tossed around the room like footballs. You had the option of going up to the dais and selecting your own, or calling out from the table what you wanted and having it thrown to you by whomever was commandeering the cuisine.

The adults danced the fox trot, waltz, tango, polka and jitterbug. My favorite to watch was the Peabody. This terpsichorean delight encompassed the entire floor, combining aerobic energy with lyrical grace. My Uncle Pro was particularly adept at this. He seldom missed a chance to get out on the floor with his wife or my mother when the band played this rhythm. Meanwhile, the children spent the whole evening sliding across the highly polished wooden floors, pausing only to eat or drink soda. These affairs were big parties that were simple and enjoyable for all involved.

One of my aunts on my father's side, Louise, was a spinster. She married at a later age than her contemporaries, who believed she was destined to remain single. One month before her thirty-fifth birthday, she wed. Having worked many years after leaving school, she was more urbane than her peers. Moving in sophisticated circles helped her develop a degree of taste and class. Her savings allowed flexibility in selecting a site for the reception. Hers was the first family wedding held, not at a catering hall, but at a hotel, One Fifth Avenue.

Her cousin Emily, suffering from cancer, was thrilled that her only unmarried cousin was finally getting hitched. She got out of her sick bed to attend the wedding. Too fatigued to walk up the steps of the church, she remained outside during the ceremony. While entering the reception hall lobby, she became dizzy and faint. Everyone assumed the excitement was too much for her. Escorted in by my Uncle Pro, she fell to the ground, cradled in his arms. It was the *Pieta* in reverse. He called out her name, urging her to come to and hold on. She died in his arms.

As a fifteen-year-old, this tragedy gave me a flood of feelings to come to grip with. Growing up fatherless in an inner city ghetto, I learned many things from my uncle. He saved my life on several occasions. Once, while in the throes of a convulsion, he stopped a car on the street, compelling the driver to rush me to the hospital.

Always in control of matters at hand, I felt safe and secure when my Uncle Pro was around. Yet here he was, helpless, as Emily expired in front of him. I saw the tears well up in his eyes. I observed, as all humans do, that we lose the ones we love. We cannot change it, so we put it aside and move on. Moreover, I learned that day it was okay for a man to cry.

This misfortune brought me to thoughts of my father. Being an infant at the time of his death precluded any relationship I might have had with him or any bereavement I could have experienced. Throughout my life, in times of need, I understood what it was not to have him and what I had lost.

Whenever the subject of my father arose, my mother would offer platitudes in lieu of any informative characterization. Her words were succinct. "He was the sun, and the moon and the stars," she would declare as she gazed off wistfully. This left plenty of ground to cover and I never gained insight into the kind of person he was. His likes, dislikes, peculiarities and biases were all obscured and dismissed by these offhand comments.

Italians of my mother's generation were close mouthed. They offered nothing of substance. Fear of outsiders, ridicule from contemporaries or society in general, the mafia and other real or perceived forces kept them from expressing and sharing their thoughts and feelings.

Uncle Pro also kept his remarks concerning my father close to the vest. "He was a great guy," and "You should have known him," and "You were cheated," were repeated chants intended to capsulize his life.

My sister and I needed more. What kept us from exploring it deeper? Was it shyness, fear, intimidation, ignorance or complacency that kept our lips sealed. Looking back, I wonder why we weren't more curious about him while growing up.

Because of the series of events that traumatized our mother, we took what little was offered on the subject, never pressing for further details. We seemed to be living under a cloud.

After his death, my mother and the family had their cherished memories. All that was left for me, to envision and embrace his life, were some old photographs and a few pieces of jewelry.

Is There A Doctor in the Neighborhood?

After that traumatic episode to restore my penis to a regularly functioning organ, I was grateful the doctor hadn't circumcised me. The result may have been mutilation, or worse, castration. My family physician, Peter Longinotti, was an alcoholic. His office was on 10th Street, between Bleecker and West 4th. After descending a few steps, which led below street level, you entered a dark waiting room and waited. The nurse was always prepared with an explanation for his tardiness. When he arrived, it was apparent he had been drinking. His heavy smoking did not conceal the smell of liquor on his breath.

After only a couple of visits, a new patient was aware that no matter what the malady, he had the remedy. His panacea for all mankind's illnesses was penicillin. This was his prescription, ranging from a simple cut or bruise, to a broken bone, or life threatening disease. As a patient, you knew what to expect. A needle in the backside for children, and a shot in the arm for adults. It may have hurt, but there was minimal, if any, risk involved.

As I matured, I questioned his reasoning in administering penicillin so liberally. What I didn't doubt was his realization that a man in his condition shouldn't be performing circumcisions. For that, I was grateful.

If one grew tired of the needle and sought a different approach, Doctor Pecorara was available for a second opinion. His office was located over the Avignone Pharmacy on 6th Avenue and Bleecker. His quarters were very unkempt. He ran the place unassisted. Dust and dirt were his receptionists. The only greeting you might receive was from his false teeth, which he often left on the table. Patients waited in an anteroom, breathing in the dusty air, until the doctor exited from the rear, ready to make his examination. Medical books and journals were stacked on his desk that served a purpose other than reference material. They provided a resting-place for his shoes, as he sat in a recliner, feet up, smoking a cigar. He may have been a doctor in the war, before going into general practice. If so, the discipline and structure of army life eluded him.

Like many of his contemporaries, Dr. Pecorara fostered the use of old home remedies. Less scientific in nature, they had some validity and comprised an area of knowledge known as folk medicine. Some of these antidotes were: taking children to the water's edge during low tide to smell the sulfur, believing it to have therapeutic properties; bringing those suffering from whopping cough outdoors to breathe in the fumes from fresh tar laid to pave the streets; administering small doses of warm olive oil into the ear canal to relieve the discomfort of an earache; and the liberal consumption of cod liver oil as a cure all for a variety of conditions.

What penicillin was to Doctor Longinotti, sulfa pills were to Doctor Pecorara. This was his magic elixir. Not as potent or fast acting as a shot, it did away with the anxiety and pain from taking the needle.

My wife Angela's father, Sam, went to him with blood in his urine, a dangerous sign of a potentially serious problem. His advice was to take the prescribed medication, and not to worry. Sammy returned after a period of time, when bleeding reappeared. Again, sulfa was administered. By the time another doctor diagnosed a malignant tumor in his bladder that had grown to the size of a grapefruit, he was given a ten-percent chance of survival. He died of cancer at the age of fifty-eight.

What I remember most about Doctor Pecorara was his sister Rosie. She was, what was then termed, "mentally unbalanced." Every Sunday she'd come to mass at Our Lady of Pompeii Church. The kids in the row would move down to make room for her two, three, or four children. She kept filing them in, and we were never quite sure how many she had, since they were invisible. After settling in her imaginary brood, she'd admonish them, from time to time, to be quiet and pay attention. At the conclusion of the ceremony, she'd stand in the aisle, directing their exit. When all were accounted for, she'd march the fictitious group out onto the street. She was known in the neighborhood as "Crazy Rosie." Some felt that label loosely fit the doctor. In an effort to economize, he'd shave off the wax from milk cartons and present it to his sister as grated parmesan cheese. I'm pleased I didn't know them well enough to be invited over for supper.

In addition to the private medical services, which were costly, my mother utilized two free city facilities. They both offered dental care and vaccinations for smallpox, polio and diphtheria.

Most of our dental work was done at 34 Spring Street, at the Judson Health Clinic. This was situated near the old Saint Patrick's Cathedral, on the lower east side. Miss Krauss was the nurse who attended to us. An extremely stern, all business individual, she was the precursor to nurse Ratchet in "One Flew over the Cuckoo's Nest." She would lead us down a long, dimly lit hallway, bypassing several examination rooms. The dental staff were young and appeared to be recently graduated, perhaps neophytes in their craft. They made no lasting impression, except that their methods were crude and painful.

The Northern Dispensary, a triangle formed by Waverly Place, Christopher and Grove Streets, was founded in 1827 to provide health care to the poor in what was then the northern end of the city. Edgar Allan Poe was treated for a head cold there in 1836. My sister and I received certain inoculations at this center. Both of these facilities are still in use.

In my early adulthood, I began going to a neighborhood dentist, Doctor Bochichio. His office was on 4th Street and Washington Place. We came to refer to his practice as the "House of Pain." Upon entering the waiting room moans and groans could be heard emanating from the surrounding chambers. My wife Angela and I were advised of his services by a family friend, Tommy Besh. His recommendation, plus the fact that his sister, Joann, was the dentist's receptionist, led us there for treatment.

We barely had our feet in the door, when she proceeded to relate an incident involving her brother's last visit. Vehemently cursing out the doctor, Joann explained how the drill slipped off her brother's tooth, cutting a deep gash inside his mouth. She failed to mention that Tommy had a nervous twitch akin to St. Vitas' dance, keeping him from remaining still for a moment. He always appeared to be on the verge of frantic restlessness. He'd stay up late at night, long after most television channels went off the air, watching static on the screen. Probably photons left over from the big bang, that static, along with other self-induced substances, had done a job in frying his brain.

Joann, oblivious to the cacophony around her, continued the tirade. Her vulgarity was not in the least tempered by the fact that the dentist, her employer, was standing just a few feet away. I wondered how he felt, standing in the middle of his crowded office, being referred to in this manner: "That fucking bastard. You Shudda seen what this jerk did to my brudda!" I guess help, good or bad, was hard to find, even in those days.

These second rate medical services were one aspect of growing up poor in Greenwich Village. There was a duality of great and vast potential, opposed by obstacles designed to frustrate, undermine, and in some cases defeat. It was an interesting dichotomy that engaged me all the years I lived there, and all the years I'd live.

The Men with the Golden Arm

Brother and the Two Rings

My cousin Jean, Sonny and Brother's younger sister, along with her then boyfriend, and later to be husband, Billy, were my first mentors. My closest cousins in age who were not my peers, set positive examples for me. Both were witty with an observant and sarcastic sense of humor. They were the first adults I observed reading books and solving crossword puzzles. Billy was drafted and sent to Korea in 1953. Six months later, I received a silk jacket in the mail. The back was embroidered with a colorful dragon. It was a gift I treasured along with my first pigskin football, which was given to me by them a few years later. These things a boy never forgets.

In addition to material things, Jean and Billy sought to give me moral direction. Sometime before my eleventh birthday, they took me to the movies to see "The Man With The Golden Arm." It was about the dangers of drug use and the horror of addiction. The screen images were powerful and realistic. However, my attitudes had already been set. There were things I witnessed, at an earlier age that left an indelible mark.

Sonny's brother Ralph was born two years after him, in 1931. They called him Brother. He was good looking and dressed with style and panache. His dark hair was brushed up into a pompadour and combed in the back like a duck's tail. His appearance, along with his shyness and quiet magnetism, presaged Elvis. The place he wasn't shy was on the dance floor. There he demonstrated a talent both sultry and sexually provocative. At times he would fall to his knees and gyrate his upper body in front of his partner. Some women were known to walk off the floor because of this. In high school, he fell in love with a beautiful, tough girl who liked living on the edge. Her name was Toni, short for Antoinette. She was extremely outgoing and affectionate. Her taste for adventure and daring was an additional attraction for him. He was crazy about her. His emotional downfall may have started when, within a few brief years, she was tragically killed in a motorcycle accident. Those who knew him witnessed the impact this had upon him.

After the death of his girlfriend, a stint in the army during the Korean conflict added to his melancholia. He may have begun dabbling with drugs at this time. When he returned home after being discharged from the army, he fell in love with a local girl, Nancy Eboli. She was the sister of one of Greenwich Village's powerful *capos*, Thomas Eboli. He did not approve of the relationship or allow it to continue. This blow added to Brother's already fragile emotional state and his addiction became his consolation. Like many others of his generation, he became a heroin addict.

Years later, while watching "The Godfather," I was struck by the scene where the Dons are discussing the pros and cons of letting heroin into their own neighborhoods. The lure of the money was too attractive to pass by. This was just about the time, the transition period at the end of World War II, that these events were occurring. The Village was one of the Italian ghettos throughout the city that succumbed to the introduction and availability of these drugs.

When he needed a fix, as part of his pool of resources, Brother would come knocking on our door crying and begging for money. "Please Wee" he'd say, imploring my mother, "I'm sick, I only need a couple of dollars." He always promised that this was the last time. "Just this once" he'd say, "And I won't bother you again." Needing all the money she possessed for her and her children's survival, my mother couldn't bear his torment and always managed to slip a few dollars under the door.

When circumstances brought us to Aunt Angie's apartment, Brother was often lying in bed, or reclining on a couch, in a stupor. Slipping in and out of his euphoria while a cigarette burned his fingers or dangled from his lips gave us concern as to whether he might set himself, and the flat, on fire. This prospect added drama to an already graphic scene. Melancholy torch song renditions, by Billie Holiday, played in the background.

It hurt to see him in such pain, overcome by his cravings and helplessness. This, along with the sadness and anguish on the faces of those who loved him, left a lasting impression on me. Ahead loomed the 1960's, which would hit hard with the sexual and drug revolutions. Many substances would be at our disposal to experiment with. I knew from these early experiences, heroin was a drug I would have no interest in.

There were few mementos handed down to me that belonged to my father. A Bulova wristwatch and two gold pinkie rings he received when he turned 21, in 1936, were his legacy. One ring was shaped like a horseshoe, with a diamond chip and his initials, A.C. The other was quite unique and splendidly crafted. It depicted a lion's head with a chip in each eye, and a larger diamond in its open jaw. It was an elegant piece of jewelry.

One day the rings mysteriously disappeared. After searching in vain, my mother came to the conclusion they were stolen. Having a drug habit, and in constant need of money, Brother became a prime suspect. Uncle Pro and our next door neighbor, Franky, called a meeting of the family and other tenants in the building. They made it clear, someone would be held to account, if the rings weren't returned. The next day they were found, thrown from the roof through an open window onto a table. This outcome was the best for all involved. The rings were recovered and no one had to be directly accused or vilified. They were kept under close supervision from then on.

When I graduated high school in 1962, my mother presented the rings to me. This was both a gift for my accomplishment, and a recognition of my impending manhood. It would take almost losing them again to realize what they truly meant to me. One

Saturday night, I got dressed, put the lion's head ring on my finger, and went out to meet my friend Shark. The first order of business was to have races in Leroy Street Park. These events didn't involve running. We'd buy a couple of quarts of Schaffer or Rheingold beer. Whoever downed the bottle the fastest was the winner. This was what we did before we were old enough to drink in a bar.

After getting a buzz, we purchased several cans of whipped cream and began spraying the contents all over the storefront windows on 6th Avenue, next to the Waverly Theater. This mischief went on for some time. Much of the froth got onto our hands and clothing. Hearing sirens, we assumed someone called the cops and high-tailed it out of there. Ten minutes later and blocks away, I noticed the ring was no longer on my finger. I panicked. I knew I couldn't go home without that ring. How could I face my mother? What could I possibly say to explain my foolish and careless behavior?

Time was a critical factor. If I was to reclaim the ring, every precious moment that passed worked against that objective. Believing the cops were there, and the danger of returning, left no alternative for me. I had to go back and search for it. When Sharky came along, I knew our friendship was solid. With the amount of people walking the area on a Saturday night, I was not hopeful of regaining it. By a miracle, the ring was still there, lying on a grating. I could feel my heart pounding as I reached down to grab it.

Was my dad watching over me once more? I felt this intercession at various times in my life, especially in my youth. From that day on, I cherished those rings. I now understood, they were my only direct link to him. My newfound respect and devotion would never again allow me to put them in jeopardy. Someday, they will be passed on to my sons. Probably, when I'm gone. I know in my heart, no one could treasure them as I do.

No Potatoes . . . No Eggs

My cousin Sonny, named Anthony, was sixteen years my senior. When I was a young boy, he began dating a girl from Thompson

Street, named Sarah. She was genuinely attractive and dressed to emphasize her attributes. Her gait had a certain air of confidence that caught one's eye. While Sarah was sexy and provocative, her girlfriend was stunning. Considered a true beauty of her generation, with dark hair and eyes, her lustrous skin and statuesque figure resembled an alabaster doll. It was obvious why they called her Dolly. Sonny's best friend was nicknamed Potatoes. He married Dolly and had two children. Like others in the neighborhood, he fell prey to the lure of drugs and became a heroin addict. Some would later question the reasons for a mature, married man, in his middle twenties, to suddenly turn to drugs. The answer might have been found in an Italian mobster named Thomas Eboli.

In those days, Mafia types, boxers and other immigrants often took on Irish names. Arriving first, the Irish already established themselves as tough guys. Newcomers emulated them, using their names or similar sobriquets, on the street, or in the ring. Eboli's Irish street name was Tommy Ryan. He was under the command of Vito Genovese and later ran the family. Vincent "Chin" Gigante was an enforcer, who would rise to prominence and head the Genovese family in years to come.

My sister and I were playing on the stoop of 15 Jones one summer afternoon, when a big black Cadillac pulled up to the curb. Out of the back of the automobile steps Tommy, elegantly dressed. His shark skin suit, silk tie, fine leather shoes and gold pinkie rings, all gleaming in the mid-day sun. He was looking for Dolly. She happened to be upstairs in my great Aunt Angie's apartment, visiting with Sarah, who was now Sonny's wife. Tommy wanted to see her right away, sending one of us kids upstairs to get her.

Potatoes' drug use continued to escalate, eroding his work, marriage and family life. Everything suffers when a person is ill with an overbearing addiction. Meanwhile, Tommy was becoming more enamored with Dolly, wanting her for his own. He was used to getting his way. The mobster may or may not have planned Potatoes demise, but certainly took advantage of his disintegrating relationships. He probably convinced himself that no one was going to miss a junkie.

One day Potatoes went to the store for eggs, sugar, and coffee. He never returned. Everyone wondered what happened to him. I often asked but never felt I was being told the truth. Maybe because nobody really knew the answer. They could only surmise what occurred. Various explanations were served up, such as, "He went to Lexington Kentucky, for the cure." This was a Federal Penitentiary that ran a dry out program for drug users that was available during this period. Hoping for a drastic reversal of circumstances, the grownups equated this with a trip to Lourdes.

Suspicions abounded, but people were uneasy and afraid to pursue any thorough investigation. I was not aware of any official involvement, or whether a missing person's report was ever filed. Most people accepted it, as they did other things, as part of life. They were simple working class folks, who didn't want trouble. Any doubts may have been put aside when Ryan set Dolly, and her children, up in an apartment in Brooklyn. Although he was married, with a family of his own, she remained, for the next fifteen years or so, a benefactor of his interest.

On July 16, 1972, Eboli was killed. The New York papers reported he was shot five times, in his head and neck, at his girlfriend's home in Crown Heights. I was nine in 1954, and Potatoes was twenty-five when he went to the grocery for the last time. He was never seen or heard from again.

Oh My Papa!

From the time I was a small child, my aunts and uncles would say I was the master of the house. I was referred to in this way, especially when being introduced to people. After reminding them of the death in the family and explaining I was the boy without a father, my relatives would turn to me and say, "You're the man of the house now."

Being fatherless and introduced that way always perplexed and isolated me. My father died when I was fifteen months old. These constant reminders only raised questions, which could not be answered. Why didn't I have a father? This made me different from others. Why was I different? I couldn't comprehend the meaning and correlate the feelings to the situation. What was I supposed to feel? It was confusing for a young child to sort out. I knew something happened to my family that was different from the others. I was basically shy and backward. This afforded a visibility I didn't care for. Undue attention and sympathy, were overbearing. The distinction of being different because I did not have a father constituted the only loneliness of my childhood.

It fell upon my mother to fill this void. She doubled her responsibilities, taking on the role of male parent, in addition to her motherly functions. A natural athlete, she taught me how to throw and catch a ball, swing a bat, jump rope, and the basic skills that became foundations to play other sports. Some kids on the block may have thought I was a sissy for playing with my mother. I learned to defend myself at an early age and most of my peers respected that. My moniker itself, was enough to repel certain challenges. In retrospect, my Great aunt did well in fortifying me with the nickname, Butch. The few who came forward were the really tough kids, who sought out others with reputations, just to prove they were tougher. Two choices evolved. You constantly fought these ruffians or made them your friends. As I grew older I saw the wisdom of the latter.

On the streets of my youth, I clung to my nickname as a badge of honor. My mother's side of the family all called me Butch. In deference to my father's memory, his mother and sisters called me Alfred. If some kid on the street used my real name, it was grounds for a fight. This nickname has remained with me all my life. It became awkward, as a professional working for the Board of Education, to be addressed by an old, neighborhood friend as Butch. The other colleagues I worked with before his arrival, looked at me oddly, uttering, "What did he say, you're Al."

I had grown into being called Al or Alfred, and was comfortable with it. If an old friend referred to me as Butch, that was fine, too. I came to accept both as equal reminders of who I was. Although, to me, my nickname seemed straightforward, I realized that others could be deceptive, even erroneous. Oh My Papa, is a case in point.

Our neighbor next door, Franky, was a tall, burly, jovial man, who enjoyed smoking cigars. He always had a smile on his face, and I never recall him being in a bad mood. He was kind and helpful. He shared his food, offering canned goods and occasionally surprising us with something special, like a steak.

Franky didn't work. He made money by taking numbers along with occasional horse bets, and other gambling ventures in the neighborhood. He kept the cash he collected hidden in shoeboxes inside his closets. Visiting a variety of establishments, he would canvass his territory, gathering these wagers. One of his stops was the corner luncheonette, Al & Ann's, on Bleecker and Jones. The older teenagers hung out there, affectionately calling the place, Dirty Waters. It had a big jukebox everyone liked to play. I was too young to participate, but on hot summer nights, I'd hear the music emanating from down the block. The low bass notes carried the farthest. I'd hear it better if my mother allowed me to sleep on the fire escape like my older cousins did. This was too dangerous, and I never convinced her otherwise. Instead, I kept the windows wide open in the living room where I slept.

Sometimes, Franky would bring us the old 78-rpm records as they were replaced in the jukebox, with the new 45's. The only significant piece of furniture I remember having in our apartment was the big Victrola. This stood between the two front windows in the living room, which also served as a bedroom, for my sister and me. This wooden cabinet stood three feet high, with a radio flanked by two speakers in the front panel. I could barely see over the top to where the records spun. After playing a selection, the needle arm would lift and another device would automatically slide the record off into a side receiving bin. For a kid, it was something to watch. In addition to having a great sound, I was impressed with the mechanics. It was the only possession we had that fascinated me.

After my father died, my mother received social security aid to dependent children. The money was less than welfare would have afforded. For an Italian-American of her generation, welfare was considered a stigma.

Somehow, we got by. She rarely worked, preferring to stay home and raise her children. Barely knowing her father, along with the loss of her mother during her teenage years and her husband when she was twenty-eight, left her a bit apprehensive. She didn't want anything to happen to her children, so she kept us close at hand. The infrequent work she did at home, making artificial flowers and stringing beads for costume jewelry, was of little financial significance, but available and popular at the time for those who lacked job-market skills.

The meals Franky provided were a treat and a break in the routine. My mother's cooking was more American than Italian, and would follow a weekly pattern. One day franks and beans, followed by macaroni and cheese, corned beef and cabbage, chicken and rice et cetera. Once a month she'd make liver, believing our diet required a periodic boost of iron. I hated the taste of it. When I was older, studying biology in high school, I was amazed how much it looked like a placenta, when served. That made my repugnance even greater.

The food I hated more than liver was spinach. Probably because I had it more often. I always tried to avoid eating it, leaving it till the end, and hoping my mother would just take the dish away. Invariably, she'd bring it to my attention, insisting that I finish my dinner. I'd chew it over and over, until it became a small ball hidden in the back of my mouth. It remained there for hours, until I had a chance to go out to the toilet. This wasn't a pleasant proposition, since it was dark and cold in the hallway. The alternative was to swallow. I consistently took the more adventurous path. As soon as I entered the room, I spit the ball of spinach into the toilet bowl. By now, all the green color had disappeared, leaving the remainder completely white. One would be hard pressed to recognize it for what it was.

I grew to appreciate spinach as an adult, but it took me longer to warm up to applesauce. When I was sick and had to take aspirins, it was difficult swallowing them whole. Instead of aiding their passage, the water or juice I drank would melt them, leaving an ugly film in my mouth. In an attempt to camouflage, my mother would crush them and mix with apple sauce. It didn't work. The combination somehow enhanced the bitterness of the aspirins. It took years not to taste them in any applesauce I would eat, even though the practice was long abandoned.

Weetsie possessed other maternal peculiarities. She was very interested in seeing the color, size, shape and amount of my fecal excretions. She would stand at attention, outside the toilet, impatiently tapping her foot, while reminding me not to flush, until she had a look. This posed no problem when I was a toddler and had a portable "potty," inside the apartment. Later on, it became embarrassing, since the toilet was out in the hallway. Nevertheless, she continued to insist upon viewing it. What qualifications she had in this area, and what she gained from her observations, was a mystery. Years later, when she continued the practice on her grandchildren, my sister and I affectionately dubbed her, "The Shit Inspector."

The fecal inspections, the spinach, the liver and aspirins, were unsettling, but tolerable. The next routine was taken from some medieval torture book. My mother would often examine my tongue for white blotches or pimples. If she found any, she'd announce, "You need a physic." Abruptly, I'd be force fed milk of magnesia. This was comparable to the aspirins in applesauce. If this didn't work, and more drastic measures were called for, she'd tell me it was time for an enema. Just hearing those words produced pandemonium and hysteria. I'd race around the apartment, desperately trying to avoid that dreadful cleansing.

My mother's generation had a fetish about putting things up children's butts. Those bullet shaped suppositories were another popular custom. Though done with loving and protective care, the enthusiasm and frequency of such practices, carried out today, might be looked upon as a form of child abuse.

Franky was good with his hands. In my neighborhood, this didn't mean that he was a skilled carpenter, or handy man. It meant he could fight. He had been an amateur boxer and my Uncle Pro would often say, "Franky could handle himself," and that he was "good with his hands." My uncle never referred to him simply, as Franky. He was always called Franky "Papa." This nickname, I thought, fit him perfectly. He was an honest, generous, sincere man, who was kind to everyone. Older than my uncle and his contemporaries, he was like a father or grandfather to those around him. That's why they called him Papa.

My Uncle Pro would always relate the story of how Gene Tunney, who came from the Village, returned to put on a boxing exhibition after his release from the army. The way my uncle told it, Franky Papa boxed Tunney's ears off, giving him a real lesson in fisticuffs. I was young and not astute enough to ask if this was before or after Tunney was the Heavyweight Champion of the World. I could tell that my uncle, and others, were in awe of Franky, and that they respected him. Being able to "handle yourself" was something looked up to and admired in a tough immigrant Italian neighborhood. They had great role models to emulate: Willie Pep, Graziano, LaMotta and Marciano.

Franky may have been as rugged as my uncle described. I had no reason to doubt him. From my perspective, I never heard him speak out of turn, or bully anyone around. He was a gentle giant. That nickname Papa couldn't describe him any better, and for years I believed in it, just the way I believed in Santa Claus. Franky Papa was a kind of Santa.

One day, when I was about ten years old, my mother was suffering from a severe headache and remained in bed. She was prone, from time to time, to get migraines. She handed me the key to the mailbox with instructions to bring up its contents. The boxes were located in the entrance hallway to the building. I put the key in, opened and removed the mail, carefully closing and re-locking the compartment. I never took notice before. It was something that didn't require my attention. Now that I was standing there I glanced over to the mailbox right next to ours. I couldn't believe what I saw. On the adjacent mailbox was printed F. Papa. What an idiot! Papa, was Franky's last name. It wasn't a nickname, it was his real name.

Many people in the neighborhood had nicknames. I just assumed, after hearing it over and over, that Papa was Franky's. I had to rationalize it some way, and later convinced myself that because there were many Franks in the neighborhood, using both his first and last names distinguished our Franky from the others. I realized from this that things were more complex than they seemed and that all things could not be taken at face value. What something appears to be is not always what it turns out to be.

Years later, when I married and moved to MacDougal and Houston Streets, there was a devastating fire at 15 Jones. My mother was away at the time, thus spared the horror and possible life threatening consequences of such a catastrophe.

The insidious power of drugs lured my cousin Brother back to the city. After living a clean life for several years, with a wife and two children in Queens, the monkey was on his back again. He left his family returning to the address he grew up in.

In the early morning hours of April 14th, 1973, Brother awoke to find the place on fire. He ran up and down the stairs, rousing the unsuspecting tenants. Despite the pain and suffering brought upon him and his family during a lifetime of addiction, his heroics that night partially redeemed him. He never conquered his habit, and died five years later of complications from hepatitis. He was forty-seven years old.

The building was ravaged. My Uncle Pro and I, along with my stepfather Al, went up to salvage what we could. The intense heat melted everything to miniature proportions. The refrigerator stood about 18 inches high. The 8 track cassettes and reel-to-reel tapes were shrunk to the size of matchboxes. There was a huge gaping hole in the center of the living room floor. The Victrola cabinet was a pile of ashes. A cedar chest, where my mother kept blankets and old photos, miraculously survived. Buried at the bottom of the console were two hand knitted Christmas stockings. My name embroidered on one, my sister's on the other. A family friend gave them as a gift when we were small children. They are unique and remain cherished items in our family. To this day they hang at holiday time in Carole's home in New Jersey.

I've seen pictures of the fire on the web, and read how difficult it was to extinguish it. Franky survived the inferno, but has been gone for many years. If the shoeboxes filled with money didn't perish, I hope the firemen found them. Franky would have no problem with that. He really was everybody's Papa.

The Last Days of Pompeii

The Crisco Kid

A catholic school education was an experience unto itself. While occurring, it is just a piece of the puzzle of one's life. A certain distance and separation of time is needed to gain perspective and fully grasp the meaning of what transpired.

The nuns taught and disciplined the student body, at times, pushing the envelope a bit too far. Hitting on the fingers or knuckles with a ruler, throwing the desk bell across the room, aimed at someone's head, or putting soap in the mouth of children who talked back, or used inappropriate language, was common practice.

Other behavior crossed the line of reason and acceptability. I was ten years old, in the fifth grade, when such an incident happened. Three classmates and I were clowning around in the boy's lavatory. Inside one of the stalls, we were all standing on the toilet seat, while urinating into the bowl. Our mischief was interrupted when a classmate rapped on the door advising us to come on out. "Sister Florinda is here, and she wants you to return to class," we heard, coming from the other side of the partition. The responses were: "Take a walk." "What are you crazy?" "You're full of shit." "Sister's not here, bug off." As the chatter quieted down, the sound of Sister Florinda clearing her throat was unmistakable. We all rushed to pull up our pants, jump off the toilet and line up outside the bathroom stall. Sister proceeded to march us back to class where we received the mandatory punishment of several slaps with the ruler across our fingers. After administering the canonical justice, arbitrarily deciding I was the ringleader, she led me back to the boy's bathroom, ruler in hand.

After entering, she directed me to bend over and administered a series of wallops to my backside. Her next directive, "Now take your pants down," startled me. I thought for a moment, then immediately followed her instructions. You learn at an early age to do what the nuns tell you, regardless of its absurdity or irrationality. In doing so, you might avoid a second beating when you got home for not listening to Sister in the first place. Most of our parents were under the illusion that the nuns were always right.

Sister proceeded to whack me several more times. There was a break in the action. Assuming she was satisfied, and believing this could not go any further, I began reaching for my pants. Her next words hit me like a brick. "Oh no, I'm not finished. Now, pull your underwear down." I froze in disbelief. My next conscious realization was the ruler against my bare skin. Years later I realized this was a violent act designed to subjugate and humiliate.

Not all my recollections of this period are dark. We enjoyed many fun times at assemblies during the year, especially at Christmas and Easter. At those times, the entire student body assembled in the church basement. The school ordered trays of pizza from the bread store down the street. Cheech and Anthony Bread were the sons of the baker. Everyday, at noon, they'd make several trays of Sicilian pizza. People, to this day, cannot believe how delicious it was, when told it was simply bread with gravy, no mozzarella. Kids lined up to order end pieces with crust, or middle pieces without. We all considered it a treat when brought in for special occasions.

Another pleasure we enjoyed was being allowed to play on the roof of the church. This happened only in the early fall and springtime, when the weather was amenable. We'd enter the roof from a fourth floor classroom. Usually, several grades were combined in play.

One spring day, when I was in the sixth grade, we were out playing on the roof. One of the boys, a fourth grader, named Joey, would solidify his position in neighborhood folklore, this momentous afternoon. Joey's grandparents ran a vegetable and fruit stand from one of the pushcarts on Bleecker Street, where his mother frequently helped out. For possessing an unusually large and long head, his contemporaries had already singled him out. "Football Head," and other mock nicknames were bestowed on Joey by his peers. The events of this day would highlight this characteristic, forever identifying him as, "Joey Head."

During a game of handball with Dom-Joe and other classmates, the Spalding bounded off the roof and onto the street. Joey stuck his head out between the colonnade adorning the roof of the church. In a harmless attempt to gaze out upon the pushcarts below, perhaps to locate the ball or view his family, fate steps in and the fun begins. *La comedia e stupenda*. Once through, Joey could not extricate his head from between the stone columns, and was trapped like a French aristocrat awaiting the guillotine. When Joey attempted to free himself, his predicament became worse. His ears began to bleed from the scraping of the stone against his flesh.

Useless attempts by the janitor to release him from his bondage prompted a call to the emergency services. Two firemen came up to assess the situation. At the same time, the nuns returned from the rectory with an industrial size can of Crisco shortening. The firemen applied the lard to Joey's head but were unable to coax it free from its entrapment.

By now, additional fire and police units had arrived, and a crowd gathered on the street. Everyone was looking up to the drama that was playing out above them. Looking back now, it was reminiscent of years later when the Beatles played on the roof of Apple Records in London. Some of the kids were now looking down on Bleecker Street with their heads between the columns, in mock imitation of Joey's predicament. This posed no additional problem since their heads were of normal size. Another battalion arrived on the scene with a tub of axle grease. The mixture of the two substances finally dislodged Joey's head from its vise.

By the time all this had evolved, our play period was much longer than anticipated. We returned to class both exhilarated and exhausted. Sitting at our desks, I noticed my friend Donald checking his wristwatch. He leaned over and whispered "Here comes the 2:09." I looked to the front of the row where Irene Pedrini sat. Under her desk was a puddle of urine, which had begun its slow descent to the back of the room. This was an almost daily ritual. Donald chuckled. Well aware of the embarrassment such a lack of control brings, I refrained from joining in, choosing to commiserate with Irene. Instead, I glanced at the clock on the front wall, checking the accuracy of the time, confirming that the 2:09 was indeed coming through. After such remarkable events, it turned out to be a rather typical day.

We would soon return to our normal school routines. Joey, however, would be immortalized as the kid who got his head stuck in the stone columns on the roof of Pompeii Church. When you said the words "Joey Head" in our neighborhood, everyone knew whom you were referring to.

Eddie My Love/
One In Five Million

The Village had its share of tough kids. Eddie Hintz was one of them. As a young boy he witnessed the shooting death of his father in the entrance to the building he lived in, on Grove Street and 7th Avenue. A troubled youth followed and the authorities often found him on freight cars and train yards, far from home. This rebellion offered an escape from his anger and bitterness. These feelings were always smoldering, fueling his torment while satisfying and enhancing his desire for adventure and daring. His quest for thrills started early.

After he attended public schools, he came to Our Lady of Pompeii to complete his basic education. Trouble, and the threat of expulsion, followed him from school to school. By nature and circumstance, he was combative and headstrong. His travails yielded some positive results. They made him a leader instead of a follower.

Quick to go off in a new direction, or first to jump into the middle of the fray, his attitude towards peril and fear was cavalier. His reputation and the situations he was involved in were common knowledge. During a school boat ride Eddie got into a fight with his nemesis, C.I. (Crime Incorporated) Hanley. They fought from one end of the ship to the other. Heaving chairs, knocking down bystanders, and trampling over and dispersing the orchestra resembled a brawl scene from a John Wayne movie.

Once while rough-housing outside Downing Street Park, a box of Ohio Blue Tip stick matches that Eddie was carrying in his pocket ignited, setting his pants on fire. A nasty burn and ugly scar on his thigh were lasting reminders of this mishap.

Upon arriving at school, he immediately organized a few of his classmates into a clique. We became fast friends. The group included Eddie, Donald and myself. The lives of Eddie and Donald would follow similar paths in the danger their pursuits provided. Eddie's choices were more in reaction to the situation life offered him after taking his father so young. Donald's choices were made to please a parent he so much admired.

In the eighth grade, Eddie convinced the coterie to join the naval cadets, to which he was already a member. The group managed to raise the money for the uniforms, which were realistic and impressive. Dark navy blue wool pants, a woolen sailor's shirt and white hat completed the kit. Stripes were added to the sleeves as one worked their way up in rank. Spats were worn over polished black boots. We all dressed with pride when we donned this outfit. Many late afternoons were spent practicing drill exercises with dummy rifles. We learned marching, and the manual of arms, at the gymnasium of Public School 3, on Hudson and Grove Streets.

Our sojourn into this world was short lived. One day Eddie suggested we go home during lunch and return wearing our navy blues. Our teacher, Sister Jean-Marie, was upset with our appearance. We were told that only the school dress code was allowed. This meant a white blouse and plaid skirt, for girls, and a white shirt and blue tie, for boys. Anything that challenged this conformity apparently was seen as a threat to their authority, and considered dangerous and unacceptable. We were sent home immediately with clear instructions not to return unless we were wearing the school uniform. Spontaneity and the parochial schools did not mix well.

Donald and I soon tired of the regimen offered by the cadets.
We quit after only a couple of months. Eddie's attraction to military
life, which offered a discipline that appealed to him, and of which
he was badly in need of, stayed on for much longer a period of
time.

Eddie, though difficult to get close to, was quick to make friends
and hang out in areas outside the small confines of the Village. He
began staying on 17th Street, and was the first to date Puerto Rican
girls. He'd come back telling captivating stories, some involving
street gangs. The rest of us wondered if he had become involved
with, or even had joined one of them. In the late 1950's, the gangs
that had been prevalent in New York City were disappearing. My
generation saw the tail end of their prominence. The future may
see them in vogue again, but in 1958, they were more legend than
reality. They were discussed and alluded to beyond their impact.
No one we knew was in a gang, still they fascinated all of my
friends.

The names alone were enchanting: The Ambassadors, Assassins,
Egyptian Kings, Golden Guineas, White Knights and Young Lords,
to name a few of the more prominent entries. The lore of gangs
from other boroughs reached beyond their geographic locations.
The Bronx had the notorious Fordham Baldies, while Queens
boasted of their Corona Dukes. Some wore jackets of silk,
emblazoned with their gangs name or logo. Others depicted
animals or symbols ranging from cobras and panthers, to skulls
and bones. Stories of these groups' escapades grew to mythic
proportions, and were greatly romanticized. We clung to these
tales, enraptured by their mystery and allure, even in the face of
the phenomenon's demise.

The school would break for lunch recess from noon to half
past twelve. Students had the option of going home for a quick
meal, or buying something locally and playing on Leroy Street
until the doors re-opened. Once during such a recess I found a
knife lying in the gutter. It was a small instrument, which could
accurately be described as a penknife. I put it in my pocket and
forgot about it. During a break in the lesson it fell out of my

pocket and was discovered by my teacher. She asked me a simple question, "What are you doing with a knife?" Why my imagination took off, I can not say. It did, and by the time this would be over, I'd realize I bit off more than I could chew. Perhaps out of boredom from the rigid school schedule, or as an unconscious attempt to retaliate for being turned away in my naval dress I concocted a story. All the folklore concerning the gangs was still floating around in my head. My response was that a gang member told me to bring it to school for a fight that would take place after dismissal. What led me to believe such an explanation would be sufficient to end the inquiry, I'll never know. Sister Jean-Marie brought me next door to Sisters Florinda and Philomena to repeat the story. Remembering the whacking Sister Florinda gave me on my bare buttocks several years earlier, I added more elaborate details to the fabrication, in an attempt to startle her. The gang member who gave me the knife suddenly became a "war counselor" and the fight after school mushroomed into a "rumble."

They listened in astonishment as I continued to embellish the tale. My intent to alarm them worked. I next found myself in Mother Superior, Sister Assumpta's office. With each repetition the yarn became more spectacular. I was becoming uneasy but still not ready to admit it was all a lie. Trapped within my own mendacious creation, the farce kept on enfolding. The next person to bear witness was the Reverend Pastor, Father Mario Albanese. His serious manner and deliberative introspection gave me pause to realize the position I put myself in. The vision of him railing from the pulpit during a Sunday sermon involving the Waverly Theater suddenly came back to me. His indignation against the blasphemous "house of sin," for showing a movie titled "The Moon Is Blue," was a memorable performance. Alternately pounding the lectern while raising his fist in the air, he implored the congregation to cast off the work of the devil while the veins in his neck seemed ready to explode from the strain put on them. His voice rang throughout the church, warning of the dangers of hell for those who did not heed his words. Mild by today's standards, the film was a saucy comedy about a young woman who flaunts her virginity.

For a Catholic in the early 1950's the blatant sexual innuendoes were in poor taste but far from excommunicable offenses. The good pastor's admonition would have better been served on his own associates. Some years later, a parish priest, Father James, ran off and married a woman he was having an affair with. Such ironies happen once in a blue moon.

To a fourth grader, Father Albanese's tirade was impressive. His passion and fury hypnotic. I looked into his eyes now and saw the same rectitude. I realized how serious the matter had become. The civil authorities were next in line and the prospect of deep trouble, perhaps expulsion, was looming. I retrenched, taking back my fable. Eschewing Martin Luther, I recanted my heresy, hoping to survive with my Catholic school education intact.

My reversal, coupled with apparent humility and atonement, was accepted and my transgressions forgiven. I learned the ramifications of telling such lies, especially to adults in authority. I resolved not to undertake anything as foolish as that again. The following year when I entered Saint Bernard, a satellite of Cardinal Hayes High School, I would find myself ignoring this dictum.

Donald attended Saint Bernard, and we remained close friends throughout our high school years, and beyond. He enjoyed fishing and a penchant for the outdoors. His only drawback in this area were the severe allergies he suffered from. This put a damper on some of his activities, but never stopped him from pursuing his interests, which also included scuba diving. His dream was to become a marine biologist and he often spoke of moving to Santa Barbara, to pursue that career and the lifestyle it promised. However, the desire to placate his father was a driving force, yet a divisive issue in his life. His father, Attilio, I believed worked for the Port Authority of New York and New Jersey. Donald held a degree in sociology from New York University, which led him to the Department of Welfare, as a social worker. After several years he moved on to become a probation officer. His plans to move to California were reduced to infrequent vacations, with the possibility of a career change becoming more remote as his entrenchment in law enforcement grew.

After leaving Pompeii, Eddie's jaunts uptown became more frequent. He was hanging out in the park where a year earlier, Salvador Agron, the "Cape Man," and his partner, Tony Hernandez, the "Umbrella Man," stabbed two people to death. During the previous decade, media coverage and access to it had widely expanded. All the sources of information sensationalized this event, making it one of the first senseless murders that shocked the city.

Dating another Hispanic girl, Eddie would go to dance parties and often return with both Latin and doo-wop records. His favorite song was the Teen Queens 1956 version of "Eddie My Love." He'd disappear for weeks, then emerge with stories and music we all enjoyed. One such record was a rare find by The Students, on Note label, called "My Vow to You." I borrowed it and brought the disc to Irving "Slim" Rose's Times Square Record Shop. Outside the subway entrance on 42nd Street, at 1475 Broadway, Slim recently opened a store that featured out of print recordings of the great vocal harmony groups from the late 1940's and 50's. His tiny subway arcade lured nostalgic kids from all over New York, inaugurating the rock & roll collector phenomenon. The walls were covered with rare 45's of all colors and labels. He was unfamiliar with the record I introduced and played it without hesitation. He liked both songs, favoring the guitar playing on the fast B side, titled "That's How I Feel." He offered me $50 on the spot. The record was not mine to sell. Slim's disappointment didn't last long. He had the record re-released, on the same label, to be enjoyed by all this music's enthusiasts. Whenever I hear these tunes played, I am happy to know that Eddie and I were responsible for their rediscovery.

After several years in Probation, Donald's job changed. He advanced to become a parole officer working with hardened criminals who'd already served time in prison. His youthful allergies developed into an acute condition of asthma. The pressures from his job kept mounting, and exacerbated his disorder. I urged him to leave this dangerous work and seek employment with the Board of Education. A position as a school Social Worker or Truant Officer was available. The latter might even be acceptable to his father, who longed to see him follow in his footsteps as an authority figure. Tillie, as he was called, must have been proud when his son joined an elite unit whose mission was to track down parole absconders. This escalation in responsibility and hazard would prove to have dire consequences. Donald sat in parked cars until the early morning hours, throughout the city's ghettos, waiting for felons to appear and make an arrest. It was a lonely, dangerous job that was literally suffocating him.

As soon as we graduated high school, Eddie's restlessness and inability to find contentment in the normal routines of life prompted him to join the 101st Airborne Division, commonly known as "The Screaming Eagles." He became a paratrooper, jumping out of planes over Vietnam.

Once home on furlough, Eddie, Donald and I got together at the Short Stop Bar on 7th Avenue, for a few beers. This was my first time entering the tavern as an adult. As a youngster, my mother, with me in hand, would often pass by on our way to and from home. A favorite watering hole of my uncles Larry and Pete, they would sometimes invite us in. These stops were brief, yet there remained for me an uneasy feeling about the place that was connected to a childhood memory.

Here, in the early 1950s, a man called, "Red," who lived with his mother and sister on the ground floor of 15 Jones, was shot dead. He was sitting on a stool when someone entered from the street and took his life away.

Except for this incident, which I held onto long after others forgot, the Short Stop was a typical neighborhood haunt. The coincidence that Eddie's father, who had frequented this establishment and was killed nearby, rattled me.

There at the bar, Eddie spoke about re-upping for another tour in 'Nam. His thirst for adventure had not been diminished by what he'd seen and been through. After leaving the service, he mused about traveling to South America to guard oil wells for $20,000 a year. Questions of how he might fit back into society were bandied around. A mercenary life fit well with his image of himself. Options for gainful employment were limited. Jumping out of planes did not acclimate one to a nine to five desk job. Police work, or any related field, was an obvious alternative. Regardless, the kind of money he was talking about sounded good. My starting salary for the Board of Education in 1967, with a college degree, was $5,200 a year. I'm certain Donald's pay at the Welfare Department was comparable. Eddie rarely played it conservatively. The trade-off of low pay for job security never appealed to him. For the time being, civil service wasn't a consideration. Somehow, Eddie would make his own way, on his own terms. He'd always done it that way.

Things quieted down. We had another round and a feeling of melancholy surfaced. Asking the bartender for a pair of scissors, I took a dollar bill from my wallet cutting it into three equal parts. We each took a piece, vowing to meet someday to reunite that dollar and share another beer together. After we left the bar, I never heard from Eddie again, and often wonder what road life had taken him down. I'm moved to visit the Vietnam War Memorial in Washington, DC, but never make it. I ask the question, "What happened to Eddie?" but keep avoiding the answer. I don't want to see his name etched into that stone. Occasionally, I look through my memorabilia stored in an old wooden chest. My third of that dollar is starting to fade, showing its age. Hopes of reuniting the three of us were dashed when I learned of Donald's death. He was staking out a parole violator when he suffered a severe asthma attack. Prior to this instance, these bouts were debilitating, but not life threatening. Previous episodes led Donald and his wife to reject the use of life support systems as the only means to keep him alive. He lay in a coma for months after the onset. Against the wishes of his parents, she gave the hospital permission to terminate his care. After his death, the father Donald so much wanted to please could not forgive the wife for keeping her promise to the husband she loved.

Statistics show that the chances of dying from an asthma attack are one in five million. Somewhere around the age of forty, Donald became part of that statistic.

The A.B.C.'s at St. Bernard

After graduating elementary school in 1958, eight classmates from Pompeii went on to attend Cardinal Hayes, an all boys high school in the Bronx. Seven of those eight spent the first year at Saint Bernard, a satellite school located at the northern end of the Village.

One late summer morning, before embarking on this experience, I found myself in the home of a school friend and fellow "Hayesman," John O'Neal. He lived in an apartment complex on Barrow and Hudson Streets that was visibly more upscale than the tenement I inhabited. At the tender age of thirteen, this Irish lad was already a seasoned drinker. It was nine o'clock in the morning when he offered me a glass of scotch. Too embarrassed to refuse, I proceeded, on an empty stomach, to drink as though I were raised in the practice. When he asked if I could handle it, I assured him of my ability. Within twenty minutes I was out cold, remaining that way for the better part of the day. I later learned that John, and others, carried me from place to place, trying to revive me. Oppressed with their burden, exhausted, and at their wits end, they placed me in the showers in the church basement, in a last ditch effort to bring me to consciousness. I came to, and returned home early in the evening.

My stomach ached for several days. From then on, I can not tolerate the taste of scotch. With a new degree of sophistication, and my baptism complete, I was ready to move on to the next level of my education. I had gotten drunk for the first time. This benchmark led me well on my way toward manhood.

The first year at Hayes, for students who didn't attend the main building, was at Saint Bernard School. Although John attended here, I had two other friends from grammar school that I was closer to. The

69

three of us made up the ABC's, Richard Artigiani, Donald Benedetto and myself. Daily, we would ride the bus up Hudson Street, or walk on foot in mild weather.

Saint Bernard was a five story structure located at 327 West 13th and Horatio Streets. A parish elementary school occupied the lower levels, vacating the upper floors for the high school. Originally, the building housed kindergarten to eighth grade. The furniture was never replaced to accommodate older students, who were by nature, bigger and taller. Unable to fit their legs under the desks, students sat with their knees spread out into the aisles. This necessity afforded some ingenious antics on the part of one particular instructor.

Brother Dennis taught history. His command of the subject seemed less important than the way he presented himself. As a model to respect and admire, he was a disappointment. Therefore, arousing a thirst for the knowledge he possessed was difficult. He'd enter the room, first period of every day, stinking drunk. His habit was dirty and disheveled. He reeked of alcohol, body odor and often from the smell of urine. He'd slur his words. It was an effort to keep up with his manic dialogue. His favorite ploy, while dispensing the history of the world, was to march down the aisles selecting a particular target, at whim. Mimicking a dog in heat, he'd lift his garment while bending down to rub his testicles against someone's knee. Trapped in desks that were made for children, the lack of mobility left us a captive audience, at the mercy of his violations. As with the nuns' mistreatment, we kept quiet and swallowed it. There'd be other ways to extract our revenge.

Artigiani was always a good student. A fine athlete, as well, considering he was short and plump. Because of this, he sometimes was passed over when teams were selected. When he sat out, he'd compensate by becoming the announcer. The numerous statistics he memorized added color commentary and depth to his coverage of the action. His knowledge of baseball and football was encyclopedic. More often than not, he did play, demonstrating skill and confidence. "Little Rich" could hold his own, in most sports.

Brother Dennis knew Richie excelled in algebra and approached him one morning during class. "There's a student who's doing poorly in math," he said, "and I'd like you to help him." He invited Richie down to his "suite" on the third floor, at the end of the school day. Warily, he agreed to show up and tutor this student.

Arriving promptly, Richie selected a desk and sat in a wooden chair. Like a stuffed pillow, his ample torso visibly protruded through the opening between the backrest and seat. Time passed, and the student to be tutored wasn't arriving. Meanwhile, Brother Dennis, inebriated and predaceous, paced back and forth behind Richie, in a stalking manner. He stooped to whisper in his ear, "You like fun sometimes, don't you?" Uncomfortable, Richie squirmed, asking where his pupil was. Brother Dennis continued his assault. He accentuated his inquiries by pinching the portion of Richie's butt that was sticking out of the chair. Panic set in when Richie realized no one was coming to learn algebra. He was alone with this madman who was pinching his ass and whispering in his ear. He managed to escape his tormentor and never volunteered to tutor again.

Richie, Donald and I stuck close together that first year. The ABC's were accounted for. The "F's", for fun and foolery, were provided by Louis Ferrarese and John Flannery, two witty, precocious, lovable trouble makers, from Saint Simon Stock parish, in the Bronx. We all became fast friends in devising methods to best our adversaries. Our generation of bright underachievers, raised irreverence to new heights. Prone to outrageous and hysterical antics, our quest to retaliate against our oppressors became relentless. Prudent and astute, we chose our targets carefully. Brother Conrad provided the perfect foil to assuage all our frustrations.

A tall man, with a head full of white hair, Brother Conrad looked older than his years. Through a teenager's eyes, he appeared to be a man well into his sixties. Looking back, he probably was a younger man who carried the worn and tired burden of his profession. He was an English teacher who came to us the last period of the day. Strictly kept in check by the stern priests and brothers comprising the rest of the staff, we recognized a weakness and vulnerability in him that we couldn't pass by.

Our taunts began with small pranks to gauge his reaction and patience. At prearranged times during the lesson, we'd all tear a sheet of paper from our pads, and peer at him through one of the holes on the side. When his back was turned to write on the chalkboard, the class would make a loud hissing sound. This unnerved him and we followed it up by simultaneously dropping to the ground books that were piled on our desks. This produced a thunderous clap of noise that caused him to jump in the air.

The game escalated when he began issuing texts for a book report. Our reading list was carefully sanitized. Only literature that had received the official church sanctions of the *nihil obstat* and *imprimatur* were included. "The Red Badge of Courage" and other traditional selections had gained this approval.

Brother Conrad entered the room visibly agitated. By now, the entire school challenged him, with each class pushing him further and further. By the time he came to us, he was a walking time bomb, ready to explode. All we had to do was light the fuse. Placing two armfuls of books on his desk, he'd walk around and stand facing the group, with sweat pouring down his forehead. He'd raise his heels up and down lifting himself on his toes, while fidgeting with the white collar around his neck that was twisted and separated from his tunic. He had a look of disgust on his face. While adjusting his clothing, he'd hold his hand across his throat turning his head from side to side. No words were spoken. The sneering, snorting and hyperventilation said it all. "Okay mess with me. Let me see you mess with me, like everybody else. I dare you to mess with me."

And mess with him we did. Students in the front row, and on both sides of his desk, would swipe as many of the books as possible. Returning to hand them out, and realizing most of them were missing, he'd lose control and scream, "Where are the books, who took the books?" Next, he'd run over to the first boy who caught his attention and slap him hard across the face, demanding to know what happened to the books. The minute the slap landed, the class would let out a loud "huh," in unison. Brother Conrad would quickly survey the room to see who was making that sound. He'd administer another slap. The class responded with a louder "huh." He'd continue wailing on one boy until he caught someone else yelling. Singling out a different boy, he'd begin the drill all over again. The class's response was the same. This routine carried on for several weeks.

The ABC's and the F's held a conference to plan a new strategy. We enlisted the help of another student, Michael Flynn, in implementing our ruse. Mike sat up front and usually was one of the first targets to absorb Brother's anger and frustration. Donald, Richie, Louie, John and I convinced him to take several blows to the face, then fall out of his chair onto the floor, and play dead. With our scheme set, we anxiously awaited Brother Conrad's arrival.

Entering the room five minutes late, with books cradled under both arms, we could tell this had been a particularly trying day for Brother Conrad. Sweating profusely, he was mumbling to himself. Following his wont, like an automaton, he placed the books on his desk and stood out, into the aisle. The books were lifted from their place and he went into a rage. He ran over to Flynn screaming, "Where are the books?" and delivered a vicious slap that spun Mike's head around. The class roared, "Huh!" He looked up trying to catch someone making that noise. He administered another blow. "Huh!" resounded throughout the room. This sequence occurred several more times. Suddenly, Mike fell to the floor, motionless, with his face to the ground. Minutes passed while Mike's lifeless body lied prone. Brother Conrad cautiously approached. The students sporadically interjected their queries. "What did you do Brother?" "What happened to Mike?" "Is he all right?" "He's not moving, Brother." Brother Conrad knelt down, placing his arms around the fallen boy, who continued to lie still. The questions from the class became more accusing. "Look what you did Brother." "You hurt him. He's not moving." "I think you killed him Brother. I think he's dead."

Brother Conrad began to panic. Tears filled his eyes, and he began to lament, "What have I done? Oh my God help me, what have I done?" At the height of his hysteria, and beyond our machinations, the headmaster came on the loud speaker with the announcement, "Will Brother Conrad please report to the general office immediately." A more propitious timing could not have occurred. Believing he had done something horrible, and that his superiors already knew about it, put him over the edge. He lay there crying and babbling like a child. Eventually they came and carried him out of the room.

The last news concerning Brother Conrad was that some students had thrown basketballs at him while he tried to referee a game. Rumors followed that he had a nervous breakdown and left teaching. The ABC's and the F's, along with most of the student body, went on to attend the main building in the Bronx. Somewhere along the way, Michael Flynn transferred and was not part of our graduation class.

The friendships that were made at Saint Bernard were intense but most would not last longer than our time together in high school. One person I would cross paths with several times over the years. He was one of the F's, Louis Ferrarese, who'd remain a lifelong friend.

Weetsie's Wedding Day

Anna Genovese being led out of 15 Jones Street by her step-father
Louis (Happy) Boitano, followed by her Aunt and bride's maid,
Frances Marone Lamarsch.

"Cheese Store,"Bleecker Street, 1937 Berenice Abbott/Museum of the City of New York

Umberto (The Professor) Canecchia with his sister, Yolanda,
a novitiate in the Missionary Sisters of the Sacred Heart.

Alfred's first Communion, second grade, Spring 1952.

The Northern Dispensary as it appeared in the 20th Century.

The marriage reception of Rita Boitano to Charles Leake, 1951.

Fire at 15 Jones Street, April 14, 1973.

Pompeii Church as seen from Father Demo Square.

PART TWO
SEX, DRUGS &
ROCK-N-ROLL

Loew's Sheridan

The Loew's Sheridan was located on 7th and Greenwich Avenues, across from St. Vincent's Hospital. Many afternoons were spent being entertained there.

Double features, preceded by cartoons or short subject documentaries, were standard fare. It was a cheap way to relax and have a good time. Watching the show while eating one's favorite candies: popcorn, jujubes, chocolate babies and bonbon ice cream, kept us safe and occupied for the better part of the day.

As a youngster I would go to the movies with my mother and sister. We'd walk the five blocks from Bleecker up 7th. There were many things to see on the way. Coming up Bleecker to 7th Avenue we'd pass Ottomanelli's Meat Store. The window was always decorated with meat and fowl of all types with lamb, deer, venison and other exotic animals hanging on exhibition. At the corner of 7th Avenue was Paganini's Music Store. Drums, clarinets, trumpets, trombones, guitars and sheet music filled the double display windows.

After turning onto the avenue, the next attraction was the grand and elegant Greenwich House. My mother would take us there during Christmas time to receive a free turkey and toys that were distributed by well-dressed women of means who attended to the underprivileged.

The Short Stop Bar and Jack DeLaney's led to Sheridan Square. At this spot stood a big kiosk at the subway entrance that sold newspapers and magazines. While traveling to Cathedral High School, my sister Carole would meet a teenage boy working at this stand who would eventually become her husband.

At this juncture we would cross the avenue passing Riker's, a breakfast, luncheonette and diner. The smoke shop on the corner of

Christopher Street advertised Optimo and Te-Amo brands, and was called Village Cigars. A life-size wooden statue of an American Indian in full headdress stood guard at the entrance to this emporium.

Up from the Square, the last few blocks were nondescript, except for one particular store that fascinated me. Just south of the theater was a taxidermy shop.

Stuffed animals of all kinds filled the store and casement windows. We always stopped to observe the life-like representations. The feathers of the birds, the eyes of the owl, and the horns of the deer, were captured in their natural movements. Being city dwellers, it gave us an appreciation of the beauty in nature and the diversity of life that inhabited the larger world we lived in. I wondered why such a place was situated here. Was it associated with the hospital or some scientific foundation? It was out of place, as were many of the pleasant surprises the Village often produced. In the flux of a big city, neighborhoods constantly change and businesses like this disappear.

The Loew's Sheridan was one of the grand theaters built by Hollywood during its glory years to attract people to the movies. The 1930's and 40's saw the rise of these magnificent structures all over the country. The most majestic were built in the large cities. New York had its share. The Roxy, Paramount, Beacon, Paradise and Academy of Music, were just a few of the great film houses. The Sheridan had a fully carpeted Grand Foyer with matching staircases leading up to the second level. There you entered the balcony through a series of four double brass doors. The large stage was adorned with velvet curtains hanging from ceiling to floor. Crystal chandeliers, descending from on high, added more grandeur to the interior design. Box seats on each side of the stage resembled those in an opera house.

Matrons were on hand to seat customers and guarantee silence during the performance. They would circulate throughout the theater reminding patrons to keep their legs out of the aisles and off the seats in front of them. Smoking was allowed in all sections and many teenagers used this as an opportunity to do something they could not yet do at home.

One memorable event was when Joan Crawford, nee Lucille le

Sueur, visited the site. She captivated everyone's attention with her stature, poise and elegant wardrobe. Her suit was complimented with matching shoes, gloves and handbag. On her head she wore a pill box hat with a small net which fell over her eyes. A fox stole wrapped around her shoulders highlighted the pearl necklace and earrings she had on. I remember standing there mesmerized. She was basically alone, without the entourage that celebrities of today travel with. She stood in the lobby being photographed, handing out glossies and signing autographs. When finished, she quietly left with as little fanfare as possible. Her being there was a treat. She had a huge presence and effect; a genuine Hollywood star of the silver screen larger than life.

In my teens, I would leave my mother and sister behind to go to the movies with my friends from the block. The route to the theater had changed. Now the walk up 6th Avenue provided more color and excitement. Across from the Waverly Theater, between 3rd and 4th Streets, was a cement floored basketball court. It was a neighborhood playground until 1962.

The Village, like many areas throughout the city, had its hoop dreams. St. Anthony's parish consistently fielded a competitive team and in 1962 won the New York State Catholic Youth Organization divisional championship. My former classmate, Richard Palandrani, with another friend and singing group member, Danny Marsicovetere, were on the winning team, the St. Anthony Mets. Danny's friend, Dapper, along with Jo-Jo Clams and Johnny Howard were the other standouts.

That same year George "Butchie" Barbezat brought one of his Power Memorial High School teammates to play there. He was just a freshman but already the star player on the team. His name was Lew Alcindor. I remember seeing him outside the park on 6th Avenue for the first time. He was talking to a girl who barely came up to his chest. It looked like he could eat a meal off a plate on the top of her head. He was the tallest boy I had ever seen, and taller than most men.

After several visits by the big fellow, the word spread and the small courts became a Mecca, drawing players from all over the city. Lew went on to play for UCLA and the Los Angeles Lakers, scoring the most points in NBA History. The record books show the Muslim name he took when he embraced Islam, Kareem Abdul Jabbar.

Farther up 6th Avenue on Greenwich between Christopher and 10th Street was the Woman's House of Detention. It was opened in 1932. On the site stood the Jefferson Market prison, part of a court complex where, by the late 1920's, only cases involving female defendants were heard. It lasted only forty years. The obsolete and overcrowded facility was shut down in the early 1970's, partly in response to Greenwich Village residents' protests about nightly shouting matches between the women behind bars and their men on the streets below. Walking by this institution was always an adventure. It rose out of nowhere into a huge complex fourteen stories high that was, in every sense, out of place. A prison this size in the heart of a small community was not feasible. This was apparent to my friends and I, long before we gained any social consciousness, or political acumen. Women routinely hung out the windows trying to converse with shady characters on the sidewalk. Cryptic, coded messages between family members or lovers and those trying to communicate with them from behind barred cells was a fascinating interplay.

On the last leg before reaching our destination was White Tower Hamburgers on Greenwich and 7th Avenue. Sometimes we'd stop there. Ordering food was a pretense for warm-up exercises prior to the show. While the cook had his back towards us, preparing some burgers, we'd squirt ketchup and mustard on the wall above his head. We always left laughing and he was at a loss to figure why.

Once we arrived at the movies, the group I was with, Johnny Santoro, Mike Sciarillo and Herminio Cordero would start the fun and games.

Herminio was the first Puerto Rican friend I had. The neighborhood kids immediately dubbed him Chico. His father was the super of 19 Jones Street and Chico helped bring the garbage cans in and out of the building. He worked hard assisting in family chores and there were long stretches of time, especially in the winter, when he wasn't seen at all. Probably feeding coal to the boiler, he would come out briefly, even on the coldest of days, wearing only a T-shirt. Longing for the warm climate of his native island, his body refused to adjust to the cold New York City winters.

Herminio was an imp. He liked to play tricks and enjoyed scaring the girls in the dark movie house. One of his favorite pranks was to buy a frankfurter, wiping off the mustard and discarding the bun. Next, he would open his fly and wiggle the hot dog between his legs. The girls, believing he was exposing himself, went into frenzy. The screams of shock and the squeals of delight were hard to differentiate. The matrons rushed over to see what was causing such a commotion. Chico would simply zip up his fly and devour the evidence.

There was a time when he got into serious trouble and had to appear in court. For the next several months, pending trial, he walked the neighborhood dressed in a suit and tie carrying a Bible and reading from scripture. When he wasn't proselytizing, the book was tucked neatly under his arm. This conduct lasted until his case was favorably adjudicated upon which he returned to "normal" behavior.

The theater provided a place to see great movies and an escape from the burdens of the world. We went there mostly in a happy state of mind, and at other times in moods of anger and confusion, seeking a refuge from our troubles.

In the winter prior to my fifteenth birthday my mother and her sister Rita went to Florida for a vacation. She repeated this trip the following June and, unannounced to her children, returned home with a husband. We had no inkling of such an event being planned or considered. To say we were shocked would be an understatement.

Extremely protective over the years, this act of bringing a total stranger into our world, without preparation, was more than unsettling.

Al, was a tall southerner from North Carolina who had been a drill instructor in the Marines for many years. Upon first meeting him, he walked through the apartment looking up and down as if conducting a dress inspection of the corps. His facial expressions alternated between a sneer and a scowl. His thoughts put in words would be "What a dump." And it was. But, it was our dump and not for an outsider to judge. Weetsie let it be known from the beginning, and at every opportunity, that we came first. This led to arguments and heavy drinking on the part of my stepfather. He was a tough leader of men who was used to giving orders, not taking them. When he drank he was resentful, nasty and belligerent. It was a tumultuous year. He would learn what Carole and I already knew—Weetsie was the boss, all four foot ten inches. Al's frustration concerning the whole situation surfaced from time to time, yet he loved my mother and withstood whatever that entailed.

Once, when he was drinking heavily, we came face to face in a challenging stare down that would have been totally to my disadvantage had it come to anything physical. I ran out of the house seeking my consolation on the street, with the friends I knew that would stand by me. My mother phoned Uncle Pro to come from his home in Queens to look for me. It was evening and his search proved fruitless. After downing a few quarts of beer, Shark and I made our way to the Sheridan to see an epic film that explored themes about the conflicts in life, but on a much larger scale. It was art depicting life, and so much more.

All of the great epics that were made in the late 1950's and 1960's were seen by me and my contemporaries at the Loew's Sheridan. The best place to get a panoramic view was in the balcony. That location afforded a perspective of what was happening both on screen and off. From that vantage point we enjoyed The Robe, Demetrius and the Gladiators, The Ten Commandments, Ben Hur and Cleopatra. One of the most memorable was Spartacus.

Johnny Howard, who lived on Charlton Street and dated a girl named Elizabeth Kilgallen, made it so. After drinking with the boys, Johnny would show up for a date with his girlfriend. She lived on Carmine Street between Bleecker and 6th Avenue. He would raucously call from the side walk, "Hey Liz, come on down." Everyone knew Johnny was on the scene. Oftentimes, she failed to respond. This prompted him to enter her building and scream aloud the same greeting. If she didn't respond or ignored his second outcry, he would then address her parents bellowing, "Send down your Daughter, I want to fuck her." This and other salutations comprised the sensitive and sophisticated Howard School of Courtship.

Johnny Howard was in the theater the first time I viewed Spartacus with my friend Shark. It was the night I sought solace from a changing world I had no control over. We were unaware he was sitting in the last row of the balcony. This was well designed to carry out his ruse. In the scene where the Roman soldiers declare they will spare everyone if the slave Spartacus identifies himself, Johnny stood up and yelled at the top of his lungs, "I'm Spartacus, I'm Spartacus."

It took awhile after that outburst for the matrons to quiet the crowd down and restore order. Consequently, Shark and I had to see the movie again to catch what we missed. It was worth the price of admission in hopes of catching another Oscar nominated performance by Mr. Howard.

To our loss, the Loew's Sheridan has gone the way of many movie houses of its kind. It no longer exists and the neighborhood lost an architectural gem along with the memories it held. It was a big part of our youth. A magical place where you became part of a dream. And, if you were lucky, you could form dreams of your own.

Thirty-five years after Al came into our lives my sister and I discussed our feelings. It was the first time we addressed the subject, realizing our reactions were identical. Al has lived in my sister's home since 1976, and they are very close.

After Weetsie passed away in 1994, there was no barrier left to separate my stepfather and me. We had grown closer over the years and there was no tension left, and no one to remind him of his position and place. We became closer than we had ever been, collaborating on many projects dear to me. As the years continue to add up, soon he will be in my life longer than my Uncle Pro, and except for my cousin Billy, longer than any adult, male father figure. Things come full circle. The man who started out as a stranger and outsider is now an integral part of the family.

Carmine Street Pool

At the point where 7th Avenue South becomes Varick Street lies a city complex containing a playing field, handball courts, a gymnasium with an indoor pool, an outdoor swimming pool and an adjoining building housing the Hudson Park Branch Library. Until graduating Pompeii elementary school, we had little use for this institution. The Catholic school had its own modest collection of books that was suitable for basics. As we became teenagers and experienced the demanding academics of High School, we began to use the Public Library more often. Our attraction to the opposite sex was a contributing factor. The girls' maturity and devotion to their studies made the probability of finding them there in quiet study more likely than an encounter at the gym or ballpark.

I'd gather with my friends, Richie, Donald and Gerard on a Saturday morning and proceed to the library to do research on a paper or project we'd been assigned. One day, while searching among the books, we discovered the "Dictionary of American Slang." We could hardly contain ourselves when we read the words it gave definition to. All the curses and off-color idioms were presented with alternative meanings. "Fuck," according to the Dictionary of Slang, meant to "plow the earth." It was a quick step for us to envision a farmer telling his wife, "I'm going out to fuck the ground now, dear." All attempts to restrain us were lost when Carla Lewis came over to ask what was so funny.

Before we could share our newfound educational insights from this erudite tome, the librarian admonished us to be silent. Carla, if she hadn't already come across this book, would have to find it on her own. She was a voracious reader and skilled researcher, even at such a young, tender age. Her motto was: "It's not what you know. It's knowing where to find what you don't know that's important." We hid the book in a place we'd remember when we returned the next time, for a more in-depth analysis.

My early experiences in going to the pool were with older boys from my block. Arthur Beretta lived at 23 Jones Street and was several years older than I. He was one of the areas premier athletes. His skill at baseball was unmatched in the neighborhood. He played center field displaying a smooth fluency in running, catching and throwing. His hitting was most impressive. He often utilized the pitching machines in Coney Island to hone his batting skills. The speed and curve of the ball could be modulated, and he became adept at mastering its variations. Once he hit the ball so far, it crashed into a passing subway car on the elevated track at Stillwell Avenue. He tried out for the Yankees, but was told he was too thin and had to put on weight. He never became a professional but excelled in any sport he attempted. This included basketball, swimming, diving and bowling. He was a natural.

His mother was one of the few Irish women living in the community and married to an Italian. Her peers addressed her, either in reference, or directly to her face as "Helen the Mick." She took it in stride, without batting an eye at the blatant slur to her ancestral pedigree.

Arthur's family, along with Uncle Pro and his family rented Bungalows at a summer camp called Ridgeberry Farm, located in Orange County, New York. It was run by a man called Skippy and Greenwich Villagers patronized the colony. Weetsie, Carole and I, would join them for a short spell. Arthur was 15. I was 11, and my cousin Jo-Jo was 13.

Arthur already smoked and dated girls. Once, after swimming in the lake, we returned to remove our wet bathing suits. Alone in the bedroom, Arthur began instructing us in the art of masturbation. I had no idea what I was doing. It was monkey see, monkey do.

Aunt Marie suddenly opened the door, got an eyeful, and immediately yanked me out of the room. She asked, with a stern look on her face, "Were you playing with your dew-drop in there?" I shook my head no. Arthur was heard laughing loudly in the adjacent room.

If Arthur had a nickname it was Artie. He was an affable character with a slight tendency towards being dense. He had been left back in school, at least once, and the three "R's" gave him trouble. I remember him calling me on the phone to arrange a get together. After inquiring where he was, Artie asked, "Where are you?" I should have responded, "Duh," but the expression had not yet been coined.

When entertaining his younger admirers, sometimes with factual stories and other times with obvious yarns, he would summon the group to come closer, with the enticement, "Have you ever heard this one before?" Thinking he might be on the cusp of finally dispensing some words of wisdom, we would gather around like sheep. Satisfied we were within range, Artie would raise his leg in the air, and to our surprise, expel a sizable amount of gas. From then on, when we were presented with the introduction, "Have you ever heard . . .," we knew what to expect. We learned to back off, allowing this caper to be experienced by any neophyte within the group.

Aside from his shenanigans, he was a good-natured guy. The same could not be said about his friend and classmate, Dennis Spano. He was a bully who enjoyed harassing younger and smaller boys. One day at the pool he began by dunking me under the water. This soon turned to rougher and more sadistic antics. He pulled me to the bottom and held me down by pressing my head against the cement floor with his feet. I struggled to escape. As soon as I reached the surface, barely managing to catch a breath of air, he brought me down to repeat this torture. Artie tried to stop him, but he would not listen. I knew if I was to have his respect, I had to stand up to him. This was a basic rule of survival I learned at an early age. I fought back, willing to take a beating, in order to show him I wasn't going to take any more rough stuff. He got the message and moved on to other prey.

As I advanced into the transition period of my teenage years, going to the Carmine Street Pool took on greater significance. Swimming, though on the agenda, was not the highest priority. We went to be seen, to show off, to meet girls and to observe the fringe element. In our neighborhood this constituted an ample group.

Danny DiRenzo lived at 40 Downing Street until the early 1960's when he moved to Weehawken, New Jersey. He was a singular individual and we were all amused by his brashness and audacity. Most found him obnoxious. He had raised narcissism to a religion. He stood about five foot ten inches and possessed a lean, muscular body. He would wear brief style attire to the pool and considered himself irresistible to women. Constantly posing and flexing his muscles, one could often catch him glancing into a store window or car mirror to revel in his reflection.

Normally, such an attitude would generate challenges. He could, however, back up his braggadocio with action. He was a disciplined amateur wrestler who had become New Jersey State High School Champion in his weight class, 127-135 pounds. He was always showing off or challenging the group to some daring deed or physical competition. He was not disappointed. Shark's strength and stamina, Gerard's speed and boxing skills and my general athletic ability kept up the rivalry. Out of mutual respect, we grew to like him and accept his idiosyncrasies.

One summer his family rented a house on Budd Lake. We visited him there. He was drinking excessive amounts of Coca-Cola and claimed he was addicted to twenty bottles a day. He grew dependent on the sugar fix and caffeine rush. Always active, he never seemed to put on any weight.

We were constantly performing feats of strength: pushups, chin-ups, walking handstands, flag poles and other gymnastic acts. This particular day a large log caught our attention and someone picked it up to press over head. The competition advanced as we challenged each other to see how far the beam could be heaved. After several tosses, we noticed a group of people emerging from their homes, some carrying rifles. Apparently, we had disturbed a property divider, instigating this call to arms. We hastily left the area before getting into deeper trouble.

Danny's career was temporarily set back when he crashed through the windshield of a car. He broke several bones and required a large number of stitches to his head, shoulder and back. While riding a ten speed, racing bike, he had entered the off ramp of a highway going in the wrong direction. When he recovered, his training became more maniacal. He soon began wrestling for the New York Athletic Club. The competition was fierce and the pressure to succeed was enormous. Shark and I went to a meet at the club, located on Central Park South (59th Street) and Seventh Avenue. We were very impressed with the facility and watched Danny compete in a losing effort to a world-class Japanese wrestler. They performed in the Greco-Roman style and many were considered Olympic hopefuls.

We didn't know at the time that Danny had embarked on a dangerous road. He was now wrestling on speed and continued this practice for several years to come. In his mid-twenties, during a match, he collapsed and died.

There were those at the pool who could swim and dive that were not content with the basic activities. Nicky Guggino, Dennis (Shark) Guglielmo, Jimmy Blue and others found more ingenious methods than the two diving boards provided. They'd enter the gym adjacent to the pool and proceed to the second floor. Opening a window and standing on the ledge proved a more interesting diving perspective for those with gumption. This was a twenty-foot drop into eight feet of water. A ten foot space between the building and pool had to be traversed, while clearing a three foot high iron rail that encircled the pool's perimeter. When kicks got harder to find, they moved this exploit to the roof of the gym, effectively separating the reckless from the suicidal. Only a handful of the older guys, the ones with the most heart and balls, or "*coglioni*," as we referred to it in the Italian vernacular, would attempt this feat. Blacky, Sallie Armetta and Luck n Lay would dive off the caged roof of the gym, forty feet high, into eight feet of water. Whether it took fearlessness or insanity, these daredevils had it in abundance.

One of the most intriguing of the fringe element was Blacky Babuta. He lived on the Lower East Side but was a regular at the Carmine Street Pool. In his late twenties, he was approximately fifteen years older than my clique. A short man, with broad shoulders tapering into a slim waist, he possessed dark hair and piercing dark eyes. Several of his front teeth, both upper and lower, were missing. Over the span of his back was a detailed and colorful tattoo of an eagle, with its wings fully expanded, flying across the moon. It was a beautiful and extraordinary work of art, once seen, not easily forgotten.

Blacky had a peculiar method of obtaining cigarette and beer money. For a buck or two, he'd challenge anyone to kick him, as hard as they could, in his testicles. After receiving the blow he'd stand grinning while collecting his fee. This sideshow became a regular attraction. We later learned a Korean War injury deadened the nerves in this area and Blacky was incapable of feeling the pain.

One day we entered the pool to witness Blacky with his testicles on top of the iron guardrail. Another man was pounding on them with his fist. Blacky sneered at one more bewildered sucker and walked away with his payment. Unfortunately for Blacky, this had gotten out of hand. We wondered what was next? Blacky completely nude and some guy with a baseball bat? The authorities wondered too. He had crossed the line of decency by exposing himself. This was a public pool with children and young girls in attendance, some with their parents. This last episode put an end to his demonstrations of prowess. Blacky, getting kicked in the nuts, was no longer a spectacle allowed at the pool.

My friend Dennis, known as Shark, was extremely bright, with unlimited potential. Possessing tremendous corporeal and mental energy and endurance, he seldom lost a challenge be it verbal, physical or intellectual. Generous, yet hard and exacting, he was at once both the delight and terror of the neighborhood. Grown men, who came of age during his time, still fear him.

As a boy he enjoyed fishing, catching small hammerhead sharks and other specimens he'd experiment with in the area of torture and torment. Because of his attraction to the predatory beasts of the sea, his angling partner "Russian Ronnie" dubbed him "Shark or Sharky."

It became unique to him alone. The neighborhood offered several "Butchies," "Brothers," "Beaks," "Cheechs" and Fat so and so, but only one "Shark." His younger brother, in deference to Dennis, was given the honorific, "Peter Shark."

Sharky was always interested in beating the odds, living on the edge and getting the most out of life. His resourcefulness sometimes leaned toward the gray areas of ethics, morality, and criminality, wantonly embracing the beat of a different drummer. His life style forsook the restraints of a nine-to-five routine and continued to develop along anti-establishment lines.

Our foray into the drug culture began simply with alcohol. We would attend C.Y.O. dances in the basement of Pompeii Church. We enjoyed listening to the music, but were shy about mixing with the opposite sex. Pints of liquor that we sneaked in would help us overcome our inhibitions. After imbibing, we would muster up the courage to ask the girls to dance. We preferred the slow tunes so we could hold them close and feel the warmth of their bodies. Once, after finding a discarded bottle of bourbon in the boy's lavatory, Father Albanese was moved to take the microphone and make the announcement, "It appears there is a Kentucky Gentleman in the house tonight."

This initiation soon advanced to include experimentation with a variety of substances. Some, under Shark's imaginative orchestration, were quite creative. A precocious, investigative mind such as his discovered the unexpected benefits contained in the nasal inhaler called "Valo." This was used to break up sinus congestion. After reading the list of chemicals in the product, Shark determined that if we broke open the plastic and swallowed the treated cotton within, it would produce an amphetamine high that would last for many hours. As usual, he was right. The taste was horrible but the effect stimulating. We stayed up for days, drinking and carousing about the neighborhood. We needed something to mellow out the nervous energy of the high, and bring us down. Shortly after, we were introduced to marijuana. As our sophistication and use of the drug expanded, we would take amphetamine and roll a pound of grass, sampling as we went along. That amount of pot in 1962-63 cost fifty dollars, yielding numerous nickel, or $5 bags, containing 20-25 joints each. This could be a lucrative business for an enterprising individual who was not afraid of the legal consequences. I never entertained such thoughts, and Shark, similar to my friend Eddie, was never intimidated by sanctions.

In 1963, my first year of college, I turned eighteen and was of legal drinking age. Our ambition was to hang out in the local bars and hoist a few with the boys. Since we were not gainfully employed this proved difficult to pursue. Without cash we were helpless. Our set back, however, was temporary.

Overnight, Shark came up with a workable solution. There was a gay bar on Christopher Street called The Stonewall Inn. According to Shark's plan, all we had to do was be friendly, make small talk, and the patrons of the bar would buy us drinks. Like most things that backfire, it sounded too good to be true. I invited my friend Richie, from Cardinal Hayes, to join us. He was a tall handsome Castilean. His last name was DeLeon. We called him "Dee," or "Big D."

He grew up on 74th Street, off-Broadway, in a middle class environment. His street smarts were not as honed as the ghetto urchins we were used to, fostering a disadvantage on this particular night. The three of us were seated at different parts of the bar, drinking and talking, for about an hour. Suddenly, I heard a big commotion on the street. Exiting the place I spot Shark and Big D fighting with a man wearing shorts and a Hawaiian silk shirt. I assumed he was one of the patrons. Entering the fray, I grabbed this dude in a headlock, lowering his frame toward the pavement. He countered by hitting me in the face with a heavy metal object. When it fell to the ground I realized it was a gun. I kicked it under a car, and the three of us took off. We raced down Christopher, turning east on Waverly Place, toward 6th Avenue. Bullets were ringing out over our heads. We ran faster. Continuing on 6th, we turned right on Carmine and headed down to the pool. Finding a window to enter, we climbed in to assess the situation and examine our options.

I turned to my compatriots and said; "What happened? Will someone tell me what that was all about." Big D explained how the guy who was buying him drinks invited him outside for a private conversation. That was mistake number one. Never separate yourself from your friends. Trying to persuade DeLeon to go home with him and "Watch TV," he makes his request more emphatic by grabbing Richie's penis. This elicits mistake number two. Instead of saying, "No, I'm not interested," and returning to the bar, Big D nails him and a fight erupts.

Looking back, it could have all been avoided. Under the pressure of the moment, with a few drinks under his belt, he probably had little choice. Moments after the fight started others came out of the bar to join in. One of them was Shark; another was the guy in shorts, with the gun. We decided he must have been a bouncer. What we didn't learn until later was that he was moonlighting, a term not yet in vogue. He was an off-duty NYC Police Officer.

Shark admitted his opponent held up something that looked like a badge. Dressed as he was, and with alcohol influencing Shark's judgment, he didn't buy it. I asked him, "What did you do when he flashed the badge?" He responded, "I broke his nose." I ventured, "With what?" Shark replied, "With this," as he held up his fist.

There was a huge gash on the bone under my left eye, caused by the butt of the gun. We decided to lay low and sleep outside the showers on the ground floor of the gymnasium building. Just before nodding off, I felt the big water bugs crawling on my body.

Awakening in the morning, I rose too quickly and became dizzy. I fell to the concrete floor reopening the wound on my face. Shark looked me over and determined I had to go to the hospital for stitches. We walked north on 7th Avenue to Saint Vincent's. They strapped me onto a table and put a hood over my head with a circular opening exposing my left eye and facial area. A nurse administered an anesthetic by injecting the flesh under the injury. A doctor entered the room with a large curved needle, and without saying a word sewed my skin together.

The police checked the hospital records and the next day we were arrested on the street. I stood out with a big patch under my eye. We found no reason to hide. They would find us if we did. At this time we were still unaware that a cop was involved. We spent the night at the Charles Street Station House. We each were placed in a 6 by 10-foot cell with a toilet and a wooden slab to sleep on. In the morning we were brought to the Tombs on Centre Street for arraignment. There they placed us in a large holding pen with all sorts of humanity: killers, rapists, junkies, arsonists, con men, flamers, transvestites, hookers, pimps, johns and queens. To add to the realism of being imprisoned, we were fed bread and water.

When my Uncle Pro heard I was being held overnight, he went into a rage. He wanted to tear the place down brick by brick, or at least, come there and "raise a stink," as he would often threaten to do under trying circumstances. My mother was hit hard as well. Aside from the worrying and agonizing, the unnecessary financial burdens of posting bail and hiring a defense lawyer was money better spent elsewhere.

The court case, which lasted over a year, became an insightful civic lesson. What was learned was the best liar wins. This cop was protecting his job. Moonlighting was illegal in 1963. He perjured himself over and over in presenting evidence under oath. The prosecution tendered the case to the jury by depicting us as cop fighters.

Danny DiRenzo's uncle, Michael DiRenzo, an established criminal attorney, represented Sharky. The bondsman recommended my advocate. What I remember about DeLeon's defense was that

Father Jablonsky, "Jabo," as we called him, the infamous Dean of Discipline at Cardinal Hayes High School, showed up as a character witness for Big D. A few years later, DeLeon's mother, who had drinking problems, accused our mutual friend Donald and all "Richard's friends" of "wanting to fuck her." That's why she claimed we came around to visit her son. Donald told me she admitted to having an affair with Father Jablonsky, at the time of the trial. Whether it was the truth or her delusion will remain unanswered. That he showed up in court is a fact. Why, will be left for speculation.

The case was eventually adjudicated. Shark, being nineteen at the time of the incident, received six months probation. Big D, eighteen at the time, was given a suspended sentence. All charges against me were dismissed. It was brought out in testimony that I was still in the bar when the plaintiff identified himself.

After high school, Big D began to drink heavily. He came out losing in his first meaningful relationship and his sensitive nature took a beating. We lost contact and I often wonder what became of him. He was very personable, extremely bright and promising and I enjoyed the years we were friends.

Whenever I pass the pool I think back upon the many memories it holds. Long after these experiences, in the late 70's, the movie director, Martin Scorcese, filmed the pool shots for his classic film, "Raging Bull," here at Carmine Street pool.

In 1967, four years after our eventful night, there was an uprising at The Stonewall Inn, giving rise to the Gay Pride movement.

Growing up here, I learned to tolerate, accept, participate and enjoy a variety of lifestyles. Intellectuals, pseudo-intellectuals, artists, bohemians, wise guys, wannabies, street punks, drug addicts, heterosexuals, homosexuals, bisexuals and all else in God's creation are historically part of the fabric that makes up Greenwich Village. Living there gave me the experience of this myriad and colorful tableau.

A Foreign Land

It's quaint to think how our lives revolved around a small area of a few blocks. To cross 6th Avenue and venture east on Houston to MacDougal, Sullivan and Thompson Streets, was like going to another part of the world. The culture was the same, mainly Italian, but it was a different parish (St. Anthony), consisting of people known only by hearsay and reputation.

My friends and I began exploring this part of the Village, mixing and making acquaintances, about the time we started high school. Until then, our lives were provincial. When I attended Cardinal Hayes in my sophomore year, it was the first time going to the Bronx on my own. My mother took me to the Bronx Zoo once when I was a child, but that didn't count. Now, I was old enough to address the larger world around me, both near and far.

St. Anthony's parish had a group of kids that made my companions look like altar boys. Every year, on the 4th of July, the place to be was Thompson Street, behind St. Anthony's Church. The local wiseguys would give away all the unsold fireworks to the neighborhood kids, who would set them off, transforming the block into what seemed like a war zone, filled with smoke and explosions. The noise was deafening, and continued for hours on end. Breathing under such circumstances was difficult. The thick air had the taste and smell of gunpowder.

Dozens of firecracker mats were stacked one upon another and lit. A mat consisted of 100 firecrackers. In effect, thousands of fireworks were erupting in a rat-a-tat pattern that simulated the sound of a machine gun. This ring, being music to the ears of the gangsters, fostered a continuous distribution of mats. The more sophisticated roman candles, rockets and sidewinders were sporadically choreographed into the festivities. Occasionally, a big blast, as if a bomb went off, could be heard after several M-80's were discharged in a garbage can.

The police would arrive, slowly driving down the block, warning the crowd to disperse. They never got out of the patrol car, choosing to give their instructions via a bullhorn held out an open window of the cruiser. That proved to be a tactical error. The more daring types would use this opportunity to throw lit cherry bombs into the back seat of the vehicle. Realizing they were fighting a losing battle, with their safety in possible jeopardy, they'd leave the scene. Once gone, they would not return until the following year. On the 4th of July, we had the upper hand.

Another place to go and to be seen was the Feast of St. Anthony of Padua. This was held every summer, becoming a show place for the local girls and a bonanza for the boys who liked to watch them. The Pompeii girls were pretty, but not as stunning and provocative as those from St. Anthony's. Each generation produced its own crop of beauties. Like Dolly before them, Gerry, Sandy and Louise were the breath stoppers of their generation. Geraldine was tall with long graceful legs, and dark hair and eyes. She was a knockout. Sandra, with her dark brown eyes, combined the beauty and cuteness of Sandra Dee with the body and sexiness of Bardot. She was petite, with long straw blonde hair that hung well below her waist. Good things come in small packages. Rounding out the trio was Louise. A sultry and statuesque brunette with big captivating eyes. In the early 60's, for callow boys attending The Feast of St. Anthony, they ruled. Meeting ones friends, having some delicious food and catching an eyeful of these *femmes fatales* were good enough reasons for crossing the 6th Avenue divide.

The feast had its downside. My first year there, in the late 1950's, I witnessed a chilling event. A black man was walking along, taking in the sights as any tourist or outsider would. This unnerved some of the locals who became irate over the audacity of this affront to their turf. According to their rules, black people were not allowed. Someone approached him using derogatory language in an attempt to instigate a fight. Words were exchanged, and several neighborhood toughs joined in. The man would not be baited so the group attacked him without provocation. The scene climaxed tragically when they shoved his head into a cauldron of boiling oil that was used to fry the *zeppole*. The man's screams were heard for blocks. He was probably disfigured for life. As a young teenager, this left a lasting impression.

The intolerance of the community was something I would have to deal with all the years I lived there. I learned through my higher education, and exposure to cultures of various ethnic groups, to escape the limitations of bigotry. Someone once said that anger was the manifestation of a limited mind, frustrated in its effort for expression. Unfortunately, the Village, at this point in its evolution, had its fill of ignorant and limited minds.

My fascination with the feast ebbed as I became involved with school, music, and the opposite sex. Information, rumor and innuendo still flowed, but the allure of being there vanished. It was said that a priest from St. Anthony's, Father Rodrick, ran away with a local girl from the parish. We were never startled by these stories or questioned their authenticity. In our reality, occurrences of this nature were accepted as customary. When mayhem happens so often, it somehow takes on an air of legitimacy.

The long time leader of the entertainment band, The Pat Laurence Orchestra, a trumpet player, had his lip split open by a brick thrown from the audience. The band never returned. Other groups tried for several years to replace them, but were not successful. Live music at the feast had come to an end.

Through the years, numerous people sang or entertained at the feast. In the summer of 1958, John Marsicovetere and The Youngtones sang their rendition of Dion and The Belmonts hit record, "I Wonder Why." A year later, Johnny did a duet with another local talent, Bobby Andriani. They sang John's composition, "I Do," which had been part of The Youngtones' repertoire. Johnny's reputation in the neighborhood was established. He had been singing on the streets since he was a young boy, delivering classics such as "I Believe" with maturity and emotion. I was mesmerized by their performance. Coincidentally, within two years Bobby would be teaching me how to harmonize, and several years after that, I would be singing in a new group with John as the lead.

Encouraged by what I saw and heard in 1960, I sang on the same bandstand with my starter group, The Influentials. The others brave enough to get up there with me were David Messina, Henry Silvera and Harold Lanza. I fronted the group doing our version of The Student's song, "Mommy and Daddy."

At one time, the feast provided a venue to sing on the bandstand and impress our peers. Due to the rowdiness of the audience, this spotlight was lost. We would have to find other avenues to meet girls and make sexual conquests.

The local maidens were decidedly intractable. Their Catholic education, combined with a strict upbringing, kept them from being sexually adventurous. A promise of marriage, after a proper courtship, was necessary to get beyond the kissing and elementary petting stage. When my generation's hormones reached full bloom, society was stagnant in the suppressive morality of the 1950's. Our first meaningful sexual experiences would occur with females who lived outside the neighborhood. The Village always attracted visitors from various parts of the city. They came to shop for leather goods, jewelry and Italian food products. They came to mingle in the coffeehouses, poetry reading rooms and the many folk, jazz and blues clubs. They played chess in the parks and attended classes or heard lectures at N.Y.U. and The New School for Social Research.

The first girls we met came from Forest Hills and Queens Boulevard. They came to visit the area and hang out on the weekends. To my friends and me, they were exotic. Most were mainly from middle-class backgrounds, living in their own privately owned homes or spacious luxury apartments. Another factor that differentiated us was religion. Many of these females were Jewish, with liberal backgrounds. Their political, social and sexual mores were less restrictive than the repressive dogma of Catholicism I grew up with. These nymphs flooded the streets of the Village or gathered in Washington Square Park to listen to music and partake in demonstrations and civic events.

Sharky and I began hanging out in Washington Square Park. Irrespective of the cultural benefits, we viewed this as an opportunity to meet and pick up girls. Our interaction skills were in need of improvement. It was time to move forward in this regard, especially since our feelings towards the opposite sex were becoming more sanguine. Boys found it more difficult than their counterparts in broaching the gap between the sexes. The comfort zone lay in maintaining separate circles where males played baseball and football, and females did whatever they did. The finer etiquettes and graces, learning to communicate emotions, understanding and sharing individual and mutual interests, are often at odds with a boy's mentality. Girls, generally being sensitive and verbal, are comfortable addressing these issues head on. Inevitably, age, maturation and bodily hormones leave no recourse than to give the situation the attention it deserves.

One afternoon, Shark and I managed to get two willing subjects up to his apartment on Downing Street for closer attention, examination and development of social and sexual skills.

His parents were away and it was a perfect chance to listen to records, dance closely and hopefully make out and become intimate in a private setting. In due time, we paired off and wandered into separate rooms.

I began kissing this girl while rubbing my knee between her thighs. She moaned and groaned as I licked her ear, gently blowing air into it. I took her reaction as a positive sign to continue and perhaps advance my maneuvers. Opening the zipper on her dungarees, I inserted my hand and began to gently caress her private area with my fingers. To my surprise and delight, she pulled her pants down, allowing me better access. She became more aroused and started to breathe heavily. I slipped off her panties and searched with my finger for her clitoris. What I encountered was disturbing. At the apex of the vagina, where the clitoris is normally located, was a long, gangly piece of flesh, hanging from her body. It reminded me of the skin under a turkey's neck that swings aimlessly, back and forth. I was more than puzzled. Having little direct experience in this area did not dissuade me that something wasn't right.

I had to step back and try to figure this out. The anatomy books I referenced in biology classes didn't examine this. Excusing myself, on the pretext of having to use the bathroom, I assured her I would be right back. I thought it wise to discuss this dilemma with The Shark!

I entered the back room, where he and his female companion were caught *en flagrante delicto*. Though annoyed with the interruption, he listened attentively to my plight, offering this pithy advice: "Put it in your mouth and chew on it."

I nervously returned, no better off than before. The wind had been taken out of my sails, and the rest of the encounter fizzled. The momentum was lost and the desire to continue in the face of such unexpected circumstances threw me off balance. For this to happen, on my first genuine sexual experience, was a long shot. I later read that this was a rare condition. She had what was termed a "hanging clitoris." My first time getting past first base and I'm faced with a medical oddity.

I was set back a few pegs in my quest for sexual knowledge. Putting aside my own frustration, I realized how difficult it must have been for her. How many prospective partners would be threatened or freaked out with her anatomical feature.

Shark developed a longer relationship with his date. We learned from Beth, that her friend became a heroin user. She died from drugs at a young age.

For my part, this experience illustrated the simple joy of being with the local girls. You knew the boundaries and there were no surprises. Moving beyond that, for now, had unforeseen risks, and could prove to be considerably challenging.

That evening I decided to go to the feast and buy a sausage and pepper sandwich. I stopped by another stand run by Ferrari Pastry Shop of Grand Street, to pick up a *cannoli*. Who knows, if I was lucky, I'd get a chance to check out Gerry, Sandy and Louise, promenading.

The Sultans of Sweet

My classmate Rocco's uncle was the ice man. He serviced the local area working from a basement location on Jones, off the corner of Bleecker. A wooden ramp served as the apparatus for hauling huge blocks of ice to and from street level. Employing large grappling hooks, similar to the tools longshoremen use on the docks, he was able to wield these chunks of frozen water. Before refrigerators came into popular use, he delivered his product to homes that still utilized ice boxes. I remember this transition period as the first of many that changed the way we lived. His other customers were the nearby merchants who operated a variety of shops and pushcart stands. One such establishment was Frank's Candy Store on Bleecker, next to Zito's Bread. Frank Gambino and his wife ran this small sweet shop selling candy, pretzels, cookies, soda and coffee. A counter with four stools offered its patrons the option of fountain service while enjoying their favorite treats. Frank would spend much of his time dispensing hot chocolates, frappes, malted milks and ice cream sodas. His egg creams where the best in the neighborhood.

A small, short-tempered man, Frank was mature in age and demonstrated little patience with the school children who frequented his store. To rush the kids along, and help them decide what to buy, Frank would nervously snap his fingers while delivering an impatient whistle. This was his way of letting us know he had better things to do. Being disturbed annoyed him, especially by children who bought little and took too much time in doing so. He preferred sitting in the back room with his friends, talking, smoking Italian cigars and drinking either wine, espresso or cappuccino. His wife seldom waited on customers and it appeared she was present mainly to cater to her husband's needs. She often was in the process of preparing food for Frank and his cronies.

Frank's impatience was somewhat self imposed. The way the items were set up added to the confusion and indecision. The counter was lined with big glass jars containing various cookies, candies and pretzels. The problem was that they were identified by price rather than by ingredients. One jar was labeled 2 cents, another 3 cents, others 4, 5 and 6 cents. When ordering a particular item, or a combination of different items, Frank would either fill a waxpaper cup or a small brown bag, depending upon the amount purchased.

I often visited the shop with Peter Vitale, who happened to be Frank's godson. Peter, aware of his godfather's intolerance, would stall as long as he could, testing the old man and pushing him to the limit. Pretending to anguish over his selection, Peter would survey each and every jar while Frank stood behind the counter nervously waiting. When he began snapping his fingers and making that whistling sound, Peter knew it was time to respond: "Give me 3 cents of the 2 cents kind, 4 cents of the 3 cents kind, 5 cents of the 4 cents kind, 7 cents of the 5 cents kind," et cetera. By now, Frank was tapping his nails on the counter while his eyes darted back and forth from jar to jar, in an effort to remember this ludicrous order. Peter continued calling out prices and amounts. Finally realizing there was no end to this pretense, Frank cried out, "Son-a-ma bitch!" and took hold of the ice pick he had hanging on the wall behind him. Raising the instrument above his head, as though it were a weapon, he chased the two of us into the street, cursing the day we were born.

In our rush to escape his clutches, we almost collided with the man who was a fixture on the sidewalk outside the store. Sometimes on crutches and sometimes in a wheelchair, he was Frank's son, Jimmy Gambino, the one-time boxer and practitioner of the sweet science.

Vincent (Jimmy) Gambino[3], the son of Sicilian immigrants,

---

3   Refer to "Warm Feelings on Bleecker Street for a Rough-and-Tumble Life", by Kelly Crow appearing in *The New York Times*, Sunday, April 13, 2003.

was born in 1932. He attended Pompeii School but his interests were not academic. He spent his youth in a boxing ring at the Catholic Youth Organization on 17th Street. He came to be known as "The Bambino," and in 1948 was a sparring partner for the great Rocky Marciano. Jimmy became a regional Golden Gloves Champion and a tough club fighter. According to local enthusiasts and followers of the sweet science, Jimmy held his own in the ring with the man who would go on to be the only undefeated heavyweight champion.

As a professional, Jimmy won fourteen fights. His first loss was at Madison Square Garden in 1951 on the undercard where Marciano defeated the great, yet aging, Joe Louis. Joe, in financial difficulty, had come out of retirement to face a man who was ten years younger. This occasion saw the defeat of both men. Jimmy, who could absorb all of Rocky's punches in the gym, did not have the will power or stamina to stay with his opponent that particular night. Marciano cried in the dressing room after administering a brutal beating to the man he idolized.

Jimmy was arrested after the fight on charges of selling drugs. He had become another early victim of heroin sweeping through the neighborhood. Due to a blood disorder he had both legs amputated in the late 1960's. He walked well with his artificial legs and regularly met with local residents for morning coffee at John's Pizzeria.

For many years, he sold socks and T-shirts from a stand he operated in front of the building he lived in on Bleecker Street, near Jones. He had a passion for horse racing and along with several friends, had a share in an animal bred for such purposes.

His life, in general, can be described as rough and tumble. He eventually stopped using drugs but often drank excessively. He died of a heart attack at 71 and was terribly missed by his friends. He was a fixture on the block and some of his neighbors referred to him as the mayor of Bleecker Street. As a kid, I just knew him as the man who sat in a wheelchair outside his father's candy store. A man who was once a boxer of some note.

Just opposite Pompeii Church, on Bleecker off Carmine Street, stood another candy store and newspaper outlet. For many years, it was run by one of the few Jewish merchants in the neighborhood, Harry Hilfman, and was called Harry's. This store carried all the candy that was popular back in the 1950's. Chuckles, Bazooka gum, Candy Buttons (colored sugar dots on paper), Charms Pops, Jaw-Breakers, Nik-l-Lip (wax bottles with sugared water), Neco Wafers, Shoestring Licorice, Wax Lips, Sugar Daddy's, Dots, Jujy Fruits and Malted Milk Balls could all be bought at Harry's.

When I became a teenager, the place was bought and run by Sal D'Amico and his sister. A woman named Anna also worked there. She possessed a berating and rather dyspeptic personality and was constantly arguing with the very clientele that provided her with a livelihood. Her skills in dealing with the public were limited and harsh. On the other hand, Sal and his sister (Sis), along with occasional help from Sal's wife, tried to make the venture a viable business and avoided deliberately alienating its patrons.

As my friend Sharky and I came of age, we had limited business in Sal's candy store. The passions of youth for such commodities sold in a sweet shop had developed into more adult appetites. However seldom we frequented the store, we managed to become friendly with a shy, quiet, unobtrusive man who delivered *The Journal American* to this and other locations. He was a man about ten years older than me by the name of Bruno Marino. His real last name was Abate, and we would eventually come to refer to him as "The Boxer."

Born in the Tremont section of the Bronx, Bruno grew up and lived in Hell's Kitchen on 44th Street. His work brought him into the Village and to some degree he hung out there. A tall, attractive man, with broad shoulders and a slim waist, he kept in good condition by the work he did and the time he spent in the gym lifting weights and hitting the heavy bag. During this time period, we began going to the McBerney YMCA on 23rd Street and 7th

Avenue to body build. Sharky was already interested in the sport. I was more fascinated with weight lifting and we learned the basic techniques to press, snatch and clean & jerk. We enjoyed the workouts. The side effect of chiseling our bodies into hard, well-defined muscle was an added plus.

We were at the age where role models affected us. We bought body building magazines and some of the early exponents, John Grimek in particular, were inspirational. Steve Reeves, who had gone on to greater fame in motion pictures was also admired. More importantly, we had our own mentor. Bruno spoke softly. He never pushed anyone around or instigated an argument. It was not his nature. We soon learned, if it came to require such action, his fast and dangerous hands were decisive. His natural build, along with the weight training he did, forged a strong body that was flexible in accommodating his boxing skills. He did not over-train, and was in no way muscle bound. Yet, his biceps and forearms were well developed and the veins in his arms were so prominent, they resembled the roots of a large tree. He wore his shirt sleeves rolled up to his shoulders. Often, there was a pack of cigarettes tucked into one of them.

Bruno would take us along on the delivery truck. The driver would pick us up in front of Sal's and proceed to the Journal Building on Pike's Slip in lower Manhattan. This was a very fascinating and busy part of the city. The Fulton Fish Market and South Street were two of the many bustling areas of trade and commerce that were nearby. Once there, we would help load the truck and begin the task of dispensing the bundles to the various locations on Bruno's delivery route. The three of us developed a camaraderie and in time became good friends. Sharky and I looked up to Bruno as if he were an older brother.

One summer day, after all the papers had been delivered, the three of us decided to go to the Carmine Street Pool to have a swim and cool off. A fight broke out with some people who were not from the neighborhood. It turned into a melee and things soon became chaotic. In the middle of the fracas, Bruno picked up the biggest ruffian and tossed him over the lifeguard's chair into the deep water. All who witnessed this feat were awed by such a show of strength.

Another brawler approached with his fists held high. Bruno assumed his stance. With the quickness and dexterity of a cat, he took a step to the side, feinted, then landed one punch that knocked his adversary out cold. His virtuosity in defending himself and delivering the conclusive blow never ceased to amaze us.

There were quite a few rugged individuals in the neighborhood. Some made their living out of it. Gazut and Sweeney were two head crackers who collected money owed to the loan sharks. They served as "enforcers" for Vincent "The Chin" Gigante, and enjoyed pummeling people. One day in Washington Square Park, Gazut went shot for shot with King Brown. Brown was a Harlem strongman who had served time in prison. During his incarceration, he worked out developing an impressive physique. He also acquired a nasty and belligerent attitude towards people in general, and white folks in particular. The liberals of the bohemian and artistic segments of the Village opened their arms to him. He despised them but took what they offered. He would soon find out there was another culture he would have to deal with.

Brown wore traditional African tribal garb with a headpiece of cloth or leather called a Kufi. This hat resembled a Fez, but was worn closer to the skull and did not have a tassel. At other times he wore a tiara or crown and carried a Shepard's staff or pole that served as a scepter. He strolled the neighborhood carrying a big, heavy office chair made of wood. He would sit down wherever he pleased and announce himself as "King Brown."

After his declaration as emperor, he would begin ordering his subjects (anyone within hearing distance) to gather 'round and heed his manifestoes. Gazut and Sweeney were within earshot and took umbrage. Brown's verbiage was inflammatory. As local Italian toughs and henchmen for the mafia, they felt their territory was being violated.

Gazut had heard enough and challenged him to a one-on-one contest. They both took turns punching each other in the face. This went on for quite some time, ending in a draw. Neither man had fallen or conceded. By the time it was over, a large crowd had gathered to witness the exhibition. Gazut had salvaged his reputation but did not walk away with a victory, leaving him somewhat embarrassed and frustrated. The next time such an event occurred, Bruno would give these professional tough guys a demonstration in the oh-so-sweet, yet savage, science.

Not too long after their fight in the park, Gazut and Sweeney were in an argument on Sullivan Street with a tall, lumbering oaf of a man. Sweeney was a short, stocky brute who could go toe-to-toe and receive punishment with any man. The behemoth they were in contention with was carrying several pizza pies that were occupying his hands. The altercation rapidly disintegrated and became physical in nature. Gazut and Sweeney repeatedly hit this man with shots that would have dropped a mule. He teetered and tottered, but would not topple. Suddenly, Bruno stepped out of the crowd, and measured his man. With one punch, the pies went flying and this gargantuan specimen fell to the ground, bouncing a few times before coming to a halt.

Gazut and Sweeney looked Bruno over. They knew he was not from the neighborhood, but most likely they had seen him around and were aware of his presence. I can not say that they admired him. Such men admire only their own ruthlessness. But, I can venture that they respected him and what he was capable of.

Bruno was a simple man with pedestrian pleasures. His interest and ambition to change his status was shiftless. He worked to provide for his basic needs. Lacking a formal education, and to a larger degree, a legitimate profession, left him with limited prospects. The thing he was best at, boxing, was merely a hobby. Some had tried to convince him to enter the ring as a professional, and offered their services as managers or financial backers. Angelo and Charlie Zito from the bread store were among them. Bruno was content delivering newspapers and when not thus engaged, could be found in the gym. Shark and I often joined him. We liked to load up on the leg press machine with 400-500 pounds and do repetitions. Bruno concentrated on his arms, curling 50 pound dumbbells or bench pressing weights that were beyond our capacity.

Bruno noticed the results we were getting from these workouts. My shoulders were broad and I had a thin waist. Shark had been body building for some time and his musculature showed it. He was better developed than I, and his body demonstrated nearly perfect symmetry.

Bruno had modeled in a men's magazine and asked if we were interested in posing for the camera. The image of our pictures in a book was enticing. What really peaked out interest was the $50 fee we would receive for the photo session.

We went to a studio in SoHo and met the photographer. He had to look us over to see if he liked our physiques and whether we were appropriate for the periodical. He seemed to have no qualms and instructed us to shower, dry off and rub our upper bodies with oil. Shark posed topless and I wore a form fitting polo shirt.

About three months after the shoot, we saw the results in a pocket sized volume. Our names had been listed as Al Steel and Dennis Stone. When the fascination with our prints passed we looked through the entire issue. The flavor of the publication became immediately apparent. It was obviously a product geared toward a gay market. This reduced our enthusiasm to show it off. We kept the book out of circulation, reserving it for our own private satisfaction. My copy was lost in the fire at 15 Jones Street in 1973.

One day Bruno came to Shark and me to ask for our help. There were people uptown who were giving him a hard time and he needed a show of strength. He occasionally hung out at Bickford's on 42nd Street and 8th Avenue. It was a self-service luncheonette on the order of a Horn and Hardart. We took the subway and met Bruno outside the restaurant. It was summertime and we were all wearing clothes to emphasize our sculptured bodies. Shark donned his ever present "guinea" T-shirt. He was known to wear similar clothing in the cold of winter.

The three of us stormed around the diner sneering, scowling and growling. No one came forward with a challenge. Bruno addressed the contingent letting it be known we would "Put the place on 14ᵗʰ Street" if there was any reason to come back. The message must have gotten across, since Bruno never mentioned it again, or asked us to make a return visit.

That was an incident in which action was not needed to win the day. When it was required, Bruno stood out. He never became a professional fighter. He never fought in Madison Square Garden as Jimmy Gambino had. Yet his skills and ability to use his hands in this craft were recognized by all who knew him.

Stripped of the Hollywood syrup, he was, for us, the original Rocky Balboa. He was our champion, like Jimmy Gambino was to an earlier generation. Over the years, Bruno and Jimmy became good friends sharing like interests and moving in similar circles.

> "In the clearing stands a boxer
> And a fighter by his trade
> Who carries the reminders
> Of every glove that laid him down
> Or cut him till he cried out
> In his anger and his shame
> I am leaving, I am leaving
> But the fighter still remains,
> Still remains."

Whenever I hear Paul Simon's thoughtful, reflective lyrics to his composition, "The Boxer," the images that come to mind are of Jimmy Gambino and Bruno Marino, who remain, two sultans of the sweet science.

Two Tales of the City

Goodnight Sweet Prince

As far back as I can remember, Gerard wrestled with demons. He was continually working out morality issues of one kind or another. He'd fight at the drop of a hat, then cry uncontrollably, lamenting the fact that he just put in tatters the clothes his father worked so hard to provide.

In elementary school he was, in many ways, more advanced than his peers. He sang, played the guitar and ukulele, and was an excellent student. Those who achieved academic prominence learned basic Latin and became altar boys. My classmates Richard Artigiani, Donald Benedetto and Rocco Iacovone, along with Gerard Madison, were in that elite group.

Like the poet Edward Arlington Robinson's, "Richard Corey," he appeared to have it all. Strikingly good looking, his shiny dark hair and eyes highlighted features that were chiseled and very European. He could have been Catalan, or Andorian, or Basque. His origins were more exotic, coming from Trinidad, via some long ago Spanish colonial expansion.

He was an outstanding track star and natural boxer. In contrast to his talents there existed an inner tension and doubt concerning his commitment, conviction and ability to live up to the expectations of his family and society in general. He had high personal standards as well.

The pressures of the outside world seemed to always be upon him, whether in actuality or perception. Somewhere in his upbringing, at home or in the parochial confines of Catholic school, he developed a demanding superego, which constantly had him at odds with the dichotomous issues of good and bad, strength and weakness, love and hate. Eventually, these forces would feed into his dark side and break him down.

The first time I remember Gerard excelling was in the summer of 1958. We had just graduated from Our Lady of Pompeii elementary school. They held a track meet at Leroy Street park and Gerard entered the 100-yard dash. The other speedsters, Shorty (Robert Raccoppi), Eddie Hintz, Leonard Besser and George Pinto, were his competitors.

At the halfway mark, Gerard was trailing badly. That's when his character and determination took over. He had great pride and did not enjoy losing. He kicked it into another gear, and at the 80 yard line, breezed past the field. He "dusted" his rivals, as he would many times in high school competition, both locally and regionally at the Pennsylvania Relays.

He disappeared from sight after that performance. It later came to light that he was sick with the flu, running with a temperature and feeling well under the weather at the time of the race.

Gerard was the lone student to go to the main building of Cardinal Hayes directly from Pompeii. At Hayes, he was a member of the track team, school orchestra and swing band. He did well in representing himself and his parish. On the home front, besides being good friends, we sang together in my second vocal group, Danny and the Sinceres. This included Danny Marsicovetere (lead), Dennis Genovese (first tenor) and Ralph Sabatino (baritone). I sang second tenor while Gerard sang bass and occasionally played guitar.

At the close of his high school career, from a graduating class of 650 students, he was ranked 31. He could have attended several choice colleges. However, he was in a serious relationship with a neighborhood girl who was a year older and more mature. She knew what she wanted out of life, to get away from her mother and the place she grew up in. Gerard started college but later transferred to a school in California. With a term left before finishing his degree, he abruptly left to join the Air Force. After his release, he married Leslie and had two children. We lost contact, and his life there was unknown to me.

The pressures of marrying young, having children to raise and support, took its toll on him. Something snapped! He may have suffered a nervous breakdown, beginning his downward spiral.

Since he did not seek medical attention, an exact diagnosis is elusive. He began to drink heavily. His marriage broke up and he returned to Manhattan.

Rumors circulated that Gerard was back, and those who saw him said his behavior was erratic. He drove a cab for awhile, but as he began to drink more consistently, steady work became unfeasible. He ended up living on the street.

I hadn't seen him for a long period of time. One day, while visiting Shark at his mother's apartment on Downing Street, I'd have a rude awakening. As I entered the foyer, a bum sitting on the hallway steps with a paper bag on his head greeted me. This derelict was drinking beer and ranting incoherently.

I made my visit and an hour later exited the building. Still drinking and babbling, this poor soul looked directly at me and asked for some money. I had spare change in my car and would return to help him out. As I walked away, it hit me. I had a feeling all along but didn't fully make the connection. I'd never seen him this bad. It was sobering and I hadn't even had a drink. I knew then, it was Gerard. The money was not an issue. I would have given him the shirt off my back, or the last dollar in my wallet. Seeing him like this, left me unwilling or unable to acknowledge him and his condition. It was a total feeling of helplessness. I walked away, not man enough to face the reality before me.

Several years later on March 17, 1986, at an age too young for such a demise, Gerard was said to have fallen down an elevator shaft. In a drunken stupor he fell to his death. Knowledgeable people, later informed me, that in one of his lucid moments he got hold of a revolver and blew his brains out.

"And Richard Corey, one calm summer night, went home and put a bullet through his head."

The Pied Piper

My earliest memories of him were with a guitar in hand. You'd find him in Downing Street Park, taking notes off a chord and arranging them for vocal backgrounds. There was a fine echo there, and we'd learn to sing harmony to tunes such as the Moonglows, "Ten Commandments of Love."

Bobby Andriani, "Ziggy" as he was called, was a master of vocal harmonization. He had perfect pitch, with a tenor voice as sweet as an angel. Under his tutelage, I learned how to sing, and was inspired to a deeper fervor in music. This interest kept me from getting into more trouble than I did on those mean streets.

After completing a song and learning its parts, Ziggy would retreat to the upper staircase, where the echo was more pronounced. Whether as a treat for the others, or to answer the call of his own Muse, he'd sing and play a particular selection, mostly accompanied by guitar and sometimes with an old piano that was upstairs. I can still hear him in my mind and know "You'll Never Walk Alone," couldn't sound any better. When he sang, he was captivating. He had a magical quality of drawing you into his world.

Ziggy was always different from the rest. A loner, who was quiet and shy, he did not believe he had any special talent. It was obvious to anyone who heard him sing and play that he was born to it. His idiosyncrasies, I thought, were acceptable because he was musically gifted. His early behavior did not alert me to the deeper troubles that lie waiting to surface.

After performing in several singing groups, Ziggy became a staff writer at the publishing firm, Hill & Range. This was located in the Brill Building at 1619 Broadway. Tin Pan Alley, as it was known, was the place where all the great tune-smiths from Irving Berlin to Leiber and Stoller, plied their craft. My generation saw Ellie Greenwich, Carole King, Neil Sedaka and Neil Diamond rise to stardom from that location. Ziggy arrived there in 1964 and became apprenticed under and writing partner of the legendary Doc Pomus. He began writing his own material and cutting "demos" to send to other artists. Many times he'd sing lead, accompanying vocals and background instrumentation, unassisted. His approach was to "work with sound," over dubbing each vocal or instrumental part as though adding another layer of paint to a canvas. The closest harmonies are achieved by singing with oneself or ones' siblings. Witness Patti Page or Mary Ford harmonizing with themselves, or the vocal blends of the Mills Brothers, Andrew Sisters, Everlys, Osmonds and Bee Gees. Ziggy became accomplished at harmonizing with himself.

The staff writers in the Brill Building, using the hits on the radio as their guide, would compose similar follow-up songs for artists in the top forty. During this period, Ziggy wrote such songs, developing his own style wherein much of the material was best suited for him. Living in a room at the Marlton Hotel on 8th Street, east of 6th Avenue, we'd often visit him there to catch up on events and hear his latest compositions. He was reminiscent of a young Mozart, without the piano. His long golden brown hair hung down to his shoulders. His blue eyes sparkled as he played, while his fingers danced nimbly up and down the neck of the guitar.

From the time he was a youngster of five years of age, he had an ear for music. At family gatherings, if someone sang off key, he'd cry. He knew it was wrong, and it actually hurt his ear to hear an off pitch. We'd often play records and try to figure out the arrangement of chords. Once, I played a classical selection by Andreas Segovia. Ziggy listened intently. "Play the first eight bars over again," he said. Invariably, he would reproduce whatever he heard. As an amusement, he'd fill glasses with different amounts of water, tuning them like a xylophone. He'd play this makeshift instrument with a spoon, hitting the glasses to produce either recognizable or impromptu melodies. Never learning how to read or write music, his facility with anything tonal was remarkable.

Often, gifts like this are not given without consequence. There were emerging signs of his abnormal behavior. He'd visit my apartment on MacDougal and Houston, claiming Bob Dylan or The Rolling Stones were outside waiting for him. Dylan did own a brownstone on MacDougal between Bleecker and Houston, but was rarely seen in the neighborhood.

On his visits, Ziggy would come disheveled and preoccupied. My wife Angela and I, would offer him food and drink. He was unkempt and at times defecated in his pants. We'd encourage him to take a bath and provide clean underwear before sending him back to his room at the Marlton. As his illness gained more of a hold on him, he began to drink heavily and take drugs in an attempt at self-medication. Unfortunately, he was never diagnosed early enough to receive proper medical treatment that may have stemmed his deterioration. He suffered from a personality disorder that came to be considered under the umbrella of Schizophrenia. By the time he was seen at a hospital, doctors claimed that irreversible brain damage had occurred. In the early years that I knew him, I was unaware he was hearing voices and that this tendency was exhibited by other members of his family.

The situation reached a crisis the time Ziggy ate glass. My cousin, Dennis Genovese, who also learned to sing harmonies in Downing Street Park, became, in later years, Ziggy's musical benefactor in promoting his catalogue of songs. Along with Dennis's own musical career, he dedicated himself to finding an audience for Ziggy's work.

After eating and swallowing glass, Dennis rushed Ziggy to St. Vincent's Hospital. The doctors determined that surgery was necessary. They'd have to operate on his vocal chords to remove the glass. Dennis, who was prone to hyperbole, became very protective, admonishing and reprimanding the medical staff. He insisted they were dealing with the greatest singer who ever lived, and he would not allow them to do anything that might damage his vocal chords and alter his singing ability.

In contrast to Dennis' histrionics, Ziggy stood quietly babbling to himself. His long stringy hair and beard were knotted and filled with lice. His clothes were worn, torn and stained. Dennis continued ranting how Ziggy was better than Frank Sinatra. At this point, the doctors and security personnel were measuring them both for straight jackets.

The trauma unit remedied Ziggy's immediate problem with the glass. They could not, however, address the long-term diagnosis of his illness. It had gone too long untreated to have a positive prognosis. When Dennis asked Ziggy why he ate the glass, he replied, "I wanted to see if I could heal myself internally."

Over forty years have elapsed since we first learned to harmonize on the streets and in the hallways. The Pied Piper of Greenwich Village still haunts the neighborhood, now, singing only to himself, a lonely tune to the beat of his own imagination. He must have several guardian angels watching over him to survive so long. He spends many cold nights sleeping on the sidewalks and eating out of garbage cans. For him, there are no comforts of home. There is no bed or blanket to keep him warm. He only has his dreams.

Dreams Lost

Irma, Speed and Mr. Hammond

In January 1964, a new singing group was formed. John Marsicovetere, singer and songwriter, who for years fronted one group or another, found himself alone and looking for a backup ensemble. His brother Danny, leader of The Marsi Trio, along with myself and my cousin Dennis, would provide what Johnny was looking for. The Marsis, shortened to fit on record labels, grew up in the Village. In 1958, they moved from Carmine Street to 4th Place and Court Street in Brooklyn. Here, in Johnny's bedroom, with a single track reel to reel tape recorder at our disposal, the journey began.

The arrival of the Beatles into the country and their appearance on the Ed Sullivan Show in February captivated us all, setting off a flurry of creative activity. Johnny composed several new songs and the group began in earnest to find and develop its own sound and groove. We rehearsed five nights a week, returning late at night to the city.

Dennis drove a Vespa motor scooter that transported us back and forth. It was a good way to travel. The speed and maneuverability of the vehicle enabled us to avoid most obstacles.

Returning late one night after an exhaustive rehearsal, we were surprised that traffic was backed up. We anticipated a bad accident on the road. It had begun to rain as we left Brooklyn and the pavement was slick and dangerous, as it often becomes with precipitation.

Dennis maneuvered between the stalled cars and the metal rail along the exit ramp on the Manhattan side of the bridge. As we slowed down to make the sharp curve, what was holding things up became evident. Someone riding a motorcycle had been thrown off. He flipped over hitting the rail, to which he was still attached. Blood was pouring out of the top of his neck where his head should have been. Instead, it had been severed off and was slowly rolling on the ground, just as we passed by. This woke us from any stupor we may have been in due to the long night. We continued to rehearse and travel back and forth for the next year or so, but nothing as dramatic as this would reoccur.

The group was working out the rough spots. The harmonies became well blended and our own unique sound emerged. This inspired additional new material that had also advanced in structure and technique. It took another year to perfect the vocals and instrumentation that enhanced our performance.

We worked hard those years perfecting the ensemble. We often left mentally and physically drained. John, the leader and most creative one in the group, however, seemed to be energized by it all. At the sessions' end, though late at night, he often took a bath, got dressed and drove into Manhattan. He would cruise the bars looking for women who were alone. If they had not met someone, this was the time they would be leaving to go home. John would be on the scene to offer to buy them a cup of coffee or provide a ride. His classic white Thunderbird sports sedan was an added lure. This system was easy on the limited time and money he had to invest in such enterprises.

I listened to the radio late into the night and in the mornings practiced on the guitar.

With a certain degree of accomplishment, we quit practicing in Brooklyn and returned to the Village. We liked to rehearse at the Greenwich House for two reasons. First, we always had a large room available to us, without any distraction. Second, if we wanted reaction to what we were doing, Freddy Antonelli, who ran the place, would arrange for us to sing live in front of a small audience.

When the Greenwich House was not available, we would go to Peter Copani's apartment on Carmine Street to practice. He was an aspiring playwright who moved in various artistic circles. At the time, he was seeking a backer for his play, "We Enter the World Crying," under the pseudonym Eric Spiros, which he used professionally. Many of his associates were gay. He turned us on to "snappers." At this period of drug experimentation, we were open to almost anything. This inhalant, amyl nitrite, was a drug that gays used to get giddy before having sex. He encouraged us to try it. It gave me a severe headache and I never used it again.

Karen Mantero, who lived down the block atop the Village Pizza, sometimes would stop by with freshly baked hash-filled brownies. That was more our style. Food and drugs together was a natural. Like the advertising slogan of the period, it was *sono buoni.*

Peter's apartment was conveniently located across the street from Lucien Barnes' guitar shop. We could easily pick up strings, picks or straps, or have basic repairs done on the spot.

Lucien left his home in Plainfield, New Jersey, to come to the city in 1962. He was an accomplished flamenco style player and luthier, who made stringed instruments in the classical and Spanish traditions. Often, we would go to the shop and hang out, smoke cannibus and listen to him play. For years, he barely eked out a living, sleeping on a cot in the shop to avoid paying rent for an apartment.

Lucien was a fine craftsman and somewhat of a visionary. He designed and developed a guitar that offered a variety of options. His prototype was a solid body electric with several interchangeable necks. This gave the musician access to the choice of a six-string, twelve-string, or four-string bass that could be slipped on or off the body at the player's discretion. Except for the drums and piano, the case stored a one unit traveling band. The idea was ahead of its time. Poor promotion, lack of financial backing and missed opportunity was its demise.

Lucien would struggle at his craft for a period of about thirteen years. Broke and disillusioned, he begrudgingly returned to his home and roots.

In January 1966, during a major strike by the Transit Worker's Union, the group's destiny would be altered. While driving for Barbazon Electric, my cousin Dennis picked up two people, a mother and daughter, on 6th Avenue in front of the Waverly Theater. He offered them a ride uptown. The woman's name was Irma and her daughter was Vanya. During conversation, Dennis mentioned he was in a singing group. He related to his passengers how he began singing at the age of ten with the Amato Opera House on Christopher Street. The woman, who was a classically trained musician, was fascinated by his story. She asked to meet us all at her apartment on 113th Street and Broadway. Her full name was Irma Jurist.

From her own promotional biography we learned about her credentials. When she was sixteen she decided to be an opera singer and turned out to be a coloratura soprano. At twenty-one she wanted to become a famous pianist. She could improvise so freely on the piano there was no point in practicing. When she was thirty she decided to become a famous composer. She wrote the first atonal score on Broadway (*Caesar & Cleopatra*).

When we met her she was in her fifties. She lived with her daughter Vanya in a large pre-war apartment that had a grand piano in the living room. We performed an original composition for her. Upon hearing it, she immediately sat at the piano and played it back in several different styles. Classical, Blues, Jazz or Pop, whichever she chose, she was a virtuoso. Ironically, her amazement was at our ability to vocalize so well, especially since we did not know how to read or write music. She often asked us where we learned our craft and we replied, on the streets and in the hallways.

To counter our lack of formal training, she taught us proper breathing techniques using our stomach muscles and diaphragms. Until now, whatever we attained came about through happenstance, rote practice and raw talent. She eliminated the variables, teaching the group to start and stop as one. This should not be accomplished from repetition, as was our previous habit, but by listening to, and following, the beat. Through these disciplines she perfected our harmonization, adding baroque styling which influenced future compositions.

Irma saw great potential in the group. She recognized the range and individuality of each of our singing voices. She enjoyed our personalities as well, and we spent time together aside from pursuing our desired vocation. One afternoon she invited us over and made a delicious Chinese meal. It was like a Russian empress working wonders in a wok. After the meal she turned to us and said, "I have a name for you Romans, The Roman Numerals." Six months later, under her tutelage, we were ready to present ourselves to anyone who would listen.

Things looked promising for us musically. We had found a mentor and a believer in our abilities. However, the pressures of rehearsing at night, attending college in the day, balancing study and the partying of street life with my neighborhood cronies on weekends, were the rivaling drives in my life. I was the only one going to college and I couldn't share or relate that stress to any of the members of my group, who otherwise, were among my closest allies.

The college regimen was an enormous load for someone as ill prepared as I was. Making it through high school by recalling classroom lessons, studying only when an imminent test or quiz made it necessary, would not suffice on this level. Poor study habits made the liberal arts curriculum oppressive. Five to six hours a night were required to cover the reading material in history, science, sociology and psychology. Written assignments in literature and composition followed. Developing and practicing oral presentations for speech class was time consuming. Mathematics, not my forte, was another burden. As a relief, I enjoyed the courses in music and art.

My junior and senior years found me participating in a variety of sporting activities held in the historic Lewisohn Stadium.

It was built in 1915 in the form of a Greek amphitheater, with 24 tiers of seats below 62 Doric columns. The stadium was City College's main athletic field with a running track encircling a baseball diamond. Lou Gehrig and Hank Greenberg played there as schoolboys.

At this location, the Physical Education majors practiced their skills and vied in individual and team events. At other times, this venue was utilized for musical concerts, graduation ceremonies and political rallies.

The class I was part of, that passed through the school from 1964-1967, comprised a group that left an impression upon the staff. Many of them considered us the best all-around athletes in the annals of City College.

Professor Frankel and Dr. Mendelis, in particular, could not recall a more talented mix in their thirty years of teaching at Wingate Hall. In recognition and appreciation of our potential they worked us harder than anyone else. They both pushed everyone to their limit while encouraging a greater effort by derisively calling us "weak sisters."

Within the bunch were high performers who responded to the challenge. Lew Weinberg excelled in strength moves and demonstrated his capacity on pommel horse and still rings. Pat Vallance was a member of both the basketball and lacrosse teams and also ran a decent quarter-mile. (I learned that as a senior at Power Memorial High School, Paddy captained the squad that included Butchie Barbezat and the prodigy, Lew Alcindor.) Constantine (Gus) Kamaras was a star soccer player and wrestler. Norman Johansen led the field in the pole vault and could not be matched in chin-ups during fitness drills.

I contributed a memorable floor exercise in tumbling and won the discus throwing competition.

My mother's early instruction and practice sessions lent me a dexterity I applied well. My teachers told me I possessed a natural ability to play most sports with a degree of competency.

An outstanding performance was limited by my average stature. My gift, if I had any, was to be able to easily acquire the rudimentary techniques in games I had no prior experience with. Once introduced to gymnastics, archery, fencing, tennis and golf, I quickly picked up on their fundamentals.

What I found most difficult was the study of a foreign language. A brother, of the De La Salle Order, tried to encourage students at Cardinal Hayes High School to study Spanish. He claimed it would emerge as the language of the future in the city. Discarding his prophetic advice, my village friends including Donald Benedetto and Richard Artigiani, opted for Italian. I, along with my school buddies, Louis Ferrarese, John Flannery and Richard DeLeon, chose French, believing it was "cool."

A knowledgeable guidance on the home front in this and other areas would be elusive. At first glance, it appears Italian might be the logical selection for me. However, my only living grandparent, my father's mother Josephine, spoke broken English to her grandchildren. I rarely heard her native tongue spoken and therefore had no facility with it. I could rely on the limited skills of various family members who had no formal training. This meant I would have to filter through their ignorance and bastardization of the dialect.

If I had the slightest exposure, I might have gravitated toward Spanish, since it has more similarities to Italian than does French. My mother spoke no Italian at all. I felt it was just as well starting off fresh in a new language. I wished myself *bon chance*, and once again, went blindly ahead into something that no one I knew could help me with.

Good direction and solid advice were hard to come by on all sides. The astute observation by Brother Robert in assessing the city's prospective bilingual needs stopped there. The Catholic school's view of the world at large was considerably narrow. If you went to college, two professions were available: teaching or social work. If you did not seek higher education, you could find employment in the police and fire departments. Cardinal Hayes contributed its share in staffing these institutions.

My sister's counsel at Cathedral Girls High School was similar. During her high school years, 1956-1960, not many women were going to college. Coming from a neighborhood such as ours was even less conducive to such a path. Those who sought an education were offered careers in teaching or nursing. The others became housewives or secretaries. In the work place, women were struggling for acceptance and equal opportunity. Marriage and raising a family were still traditionally preferable.

There were not an overwhelming array of choices and no one to offer alternatives. A handful of family members were lucky enough to finish high school. The women all stayed home to tend to domestic chores. The males were mostly truck drivers.

The business world as well as any professional or academic advancement were foreign to my background.

My mother had her own ideas. She stepped forward to see them through. Unskilled and uneducated and forced by circumstances to raise two children alone, Weetsie put her foot down. She insisted that my sister go to college, and had this in mind long before the actual time it would occur. Bitter lessons drove her to insure that Carole would be independent and solvent. An education, she believed, would give her that status. Carole would be able to make ends meet with or without a man. Weetsie had no idea what the term "economic empowerment" meant, but she knew she was doing the right thing. Less forceful with me, believing a man could make his own way, she let me decide my own fate.

My sister pioneered the road to college and I saw that it was possible. We were both lucky to gain entrance to the City College system, where tuition was free. We owed a debt to the city we loved. By allowing Carole to attend Hunter College and myself enrolled in City College, we embarked on a journey that would change our lives. We paid back this obligation by devoting ourselves to the public schools and servicing the children of the city for our entire working careers.

My musical ear, however, never carried over to the study of language and I was terribly handicapped. After two years of high school and two terms of college French, I was at a loss to verbally communicate or orally grasp the spoken word. The fluency of *La Langue Francais*, was baffling. I could not distinguished where one phrase ended and the next began. It was a wonderfully melodic flow that left me speechless.

Lois Frisher and Phyllis Newman were my saviors. They were two bright, good looking young women who were always well prepared. We sat together in the back of the room in all of our French courses. They routinely bailed me out by interpreting the professor's instructions, especially when he was addressing me. *"Monsieur Canecchia, ferme la fenêtre, s'il vous plait."* The girls would whisper, "Al, close the window." *"Monsieur Canecchia, ouvre le livre a la page soixante-neuf."* This brought a smile to my face upon translation. The ladies were not surprised that I managed to recall the word sixty-nine.

The frequent assistance was all done under their breath. Whether the instructor realized or not that I was being fed the information, he pretended like I understood him. When he tried to engage me in deeper conversation, I was really at a loss. It was obvious that he was dealing with someone who was in over his head. I made up this deficiency by studying hard and doing well on the written exams. I eventually became proficient in reading the language. In the final term, novels, such as *L'Etranger* by Albert Camus, and plays including Jean Anouilh's, *Antigone*, were read entirely in the original. I regret that I did not maintain this skill.

I was grateful that Phyllis and Lois were there to help me along. I was surviving in all my subjects while accruing valuable credits toward a degree.

I always had friends who took kindly to me and assisted me in making the grade. In elementary school, Joan Pepia, served the same purpose of keeping me abreast of the on going lessons. She sat directly in front of me and I often peered over her shoulder to check the correct answers to written examinations.

My mind constantly drifted off to places and things removed from the classroom. These were not lofty or important concerns that drew me away but momentary escapes from the mundane realities of life.

My preoccupations led the nuns to believe I was not up to the tasks before me. They had little faith in my ability to do well in school. I exhibited signs of having Attention Deficit Disorder before it became part of the lexicon.

In time, I would prove the sisiers wrong. As I advanced further into high school I began to take my studies more seriously, and would ultimately complete my higher education.

Although things looked good from one aspect, they were approaching shaky ground on another. My drug experimentation was reaching new levels. Methedrine, a pure crystal form of amphetamine, caught Shark's attention, and we began to dabble in it. Eventually, Sharky was instructed by "The Doctor" Paulie Matura in how to shoot up. The first time I allowed him to administer to me in this way, I was high for three days. It's immediately apparent why addicts prefer mainlining. The rush is unbelievable. The short delay it takes to travel from the center of your arm to your brain, makes the drugs impact almost immediate, culminating in an explosion of energy, light, thought and creativity.

Like Dorothy opening the door to Oz, everything is changed. The world is full of color, brightness, music and dance. You feel light as a feather and ready to soar. It is difficult to view things through the same lens again.

The impact of the drug is so powerful that, at first, you have to recline until your body makes an adjustment. Heart rate accelerates, stimuli are taken in rapid succession, while thoughts rush through your mind at a frantic pace. You are a superman. Nothing seems beyond your grasp. My guitar playing and singing leapt in endurance. I stood on the corner of Carmine and Bedford Streets playing and singing with tireless abandon.

This effect was wonderful until it began to wear off. The down side included irritability, lack of concentration and eventual exhaustion leading to depression. I could tell from the beginning where this cycle might lead. I would have to be careful. This was a dangerous drug.

Shark visited Irma's place to hear the latest songs. We both went into the bathroom to do speed. She was pleased with how the group was progressing and set up an audition with John Hammond Sr., of Columbia Records. He had "discovered" everyone from Benny Goodman and Billy Holiday, to Bob Dylan and beyond. Irma had a history with him that was unclear to the group, and would end up not being an asset for us. She simply stated he was a friend, and he was willing to hear us perform in his office at the CBS building, on 52nd Street and 6th Avenue.

We prepared our best material and with a couple of acoustic guitars entered his private chamber. He was very business like, stern, with no hint of cordiality. We were barely into our first number when he interrupted, stating, "Those guitars are out of tune."

Johnny, our lead singer, was a professional who already had cut seven records totaling fourteen sides. He rarely, if ever, sang off key. These recordings were all made before electronic advances could adjust and correct a flat or sharp note. He sang with a full orchestra, and was used to delivering the song as many times as needed, until the producer got what he believed to be the "perfect" take. Johnny knew how to deliver a song. Yet, I never saw him so thrown off or unglued. His look of embarrassment gave way to fear, and if there were a hole in the wall to crawl into, he would have.

Dennis had close to perfect pitch. He arranged the basic vocal harmonies with added suggestions from Irma. We had previously tuned the instruments to concert. There was a piano in the room that verified our position. No one else, including Irma, who did have perfect pitch, heard an out of tune guitar. Yet, Mr. Hammond was adamant, becoming more emphatic in his insistence. His stubbornness stymied us. The average age of the group was twenty-one, and we were startled and discouraged by his dismissive manner. In short, we fell apart. We kept fumbling with the pegs, in useless attempts to retune the instruments to his satisfaction. He gave a vivid demonstration of the power of a man in his position to unnerve and sabotage.

Our confidence shaken, he refused to let us get through a single song. He kept interrupting, saying, "Next tune please." We responded as best we could. It was obvious he didn't want to give us a chance. He turned to Irma, saying, "Why did you bother me? This is not ready." We left there defeated.

Not a word was spoken on the elevator ride down to the street. We boarded a taxi, the four of us in the back, with Irma up front with the driver. She turned, holding her hand in front of her eyes and pulling it slowly down. Her words were, "I have egg on my face." We recovered enough to analyze the situation. The guitars were not the problem. We all knew they were properly tuned. John Hammond was the culprit, and we told her so. She considered this for a moment, then responded, "That son of a bitch."

John Hammond was getting even with Irma for something, personal or professional, which had nothing to do with The Roman Numerals. After voicing our opinions, it was a long, quiet ride back to Irma's apartment. We regretted disappointing her, but knew in our hearts, we were not to blame. A year later we would sign a recording contract with Columbia Records. Mr. Hammond had no involvement in our vindication.

The shooting of speed had come to a crisis point for me. Moving beyond my initiation with the drug, I was at a crossroads. If I continued, there was the possibility of losing control. The last episode, at Shark's cousin Mary Jo's home in Hempstead, Long Island, was my epiphany.

Shark previously introduced me to Mary Jo and we spoke briefly on the sidewalk outside of his apartment building. We were attracted to one another but nothing serious developed. She lived far away and I did not have a car. We were at the age where we were experimenting with sex and drugs.

At the house, the girls talked in the kitchen while the guys went down to the lower level. Shark prepared the syringe. He had his belt twisted tightly around my upper arm while searching for my vein. Several attempts to inject me had missed the mark. He was not as adept with the needle as he would later become. Because of the failed punctures, blood was dripping from my arm. I became dizzy due to the lack of oxygen to my brain. We were in the bathroom in the basement. A woman who rented rooms there, came out to question what the loud thud she heard was. That was me, passing out and falling to the floor. Shark placated her by saying I had an asthma attack and would soon recover. When I came to, I drank the mixture. That was the last time I used speed, or the paraphernalia for its delivery.

We returned upstairs. Dennis and Beth disappeared into the back rooms. Mary Jo and I started making out on the couch. She was wearing a sweater with tights that complimented her figure. I was so wired by the speed that it was difficult to become aroused. I decided to lie between her legs. The boundless energy generated by the drug kept me persevering there. When I came up for air, I noticed her clothing was spotted with a mixture of my saliva and her juices. Wrapt in each other's arms, her essence lingering upon me, my heart pounded like a jack-hammer. Mary Jo dozed off in tranquillity. Incalculable thoughts ran furiously through my head. I knew I'd be up for days.

In the years to come, Beth would develop a dependency on pills. Mary Jo's life would take a more sinister turn.

A short time after our encounter, I ran into Mary Jo outside John's Pizzeria. We shared an awkward moment recalling our frenzied liaison.

That was the last time I would see her. Two years later, while traveling by car from San Francisco to the East Coast for the purpose of getting married, Mary Jo and her boyfriend, Roy, were murdered. She was taken away at nineteen years old, in the prime of her youth. Whether a drug deal gone wrong or the brutal act of a lunatic is still in question. The case remains unsolved.

The image of the neighborhood littered with junkies, from my early youth, remained a strong prohibitive. If not stumbling down the street, they'd nod off in the middle of a sentence. When more engaged, they'd rant on in an endless babble of incoherent nonsense. At the time, my friends and I found it amusing. It would not be so, whether in an up or down state, if I ended up addicted like those druggies I once goofed on.

Continuing down the path I was on would be self-destructive. Others used drugs for years to come, and suffered the consequences. Some paid the ultimate price. Those who survive never gain total victory. They never entirely kill the beast. They must be vigilant the rest of their lives, for it is always lurking in the shadows. I didn't want to be at the mercy of something bigger than myself. It was a relatively short journey, but the speed train had come to its last stop.

My cousin Dennis caught up with Irma in 1975, about ten years after our audition with John Hammond. He visited with her in her old apartment on the Upper West Side, to seek her opinion and perhaps her involvement in his latest musical project. She was chirping like a bird, making t-t-t-t—stuttering articulations in a ludicrous manner. She talked about the Holy Ghost while making these strange and comical sounds. She sat at the piano amid her chatter. She was alone in her own world. Dennis left, taking with him another lost dream.

That Long and Winding Road

"Stay away from Johnny Mouse. He's bad luck." That's what Eddie Hilly would tell me and my cousin Dennis whenever we'd run into him in Leroy Street Park. Every summer you could find him there drinking beer and telling his life story.

He started out as just another neighborhood kid with a dream; a tough Irish street lad who wanted to be a professional boxer, and was good enough to be in The Golden Gloves. His girlfriend for a short period of time was the beautiful Louise from St. Anthony's. She was one of the trio of beauties that drew boys from all over the neighborhood to the feast. The story Eddie told was a combination of a serious career ending lip injury and unrequited love that destroyed his dreams and led him to use and abuse drugs. Cheap booze and beer followed years of heroin use. At times you'd find Eddie and Jimmy Blue on the Bowery and Houston Streets. They'd be cleaning car windshields for whatever change people would give them. They were the forerunners of the present day "squeegee" men.

There were so many similar stories in the neighborhood that left doubt whether drugs had precipitated one's downfall, or had been turned to in response to the vicissitudes of life. What was certain was, if it was summertime, Eddie Hilly would be in the park drinking beer. There was no argument about that. Where he went in the winter was a mystery. No one seemed to know. He just disappeared.

In the winter of 1967, Columbia released the record, "Matchstick in A Whirlpool," by The Roman Numerals. Our promoter and financial backer, Peter Steinmann, along with the record company, arranged to fly the group to Cleveland, Ohio to appear on The Up-Beat Show.

Peter's father, a merchant in the produce market, saved ten thousand dollars over a lifetime to invest as speculation. He parlayed that amount into ten million by backing several movies that became huge hits. "The Umbrellas of Cherbourg" and "The Pawn Broker," were two of the productions that helped make him a wealthy man. The Steinmanns lived in a four-story townhouse on 83rd Street between 5th and Madison, a block away from The Metropolitan Museum of Art. Their home was filled with fine paintings and sculpture, befitting their status. It was very impressive for four young men to see how people with money lived. It gave hope to the American dream. They were not born rich. They did it the old fashioned way, they earned it. With their help maybe we could attain such heights.

The elder Steinmann gave Peter the exact amount that he started out with, telling his son, "Here is the chance to do what I did. You will make it or break it on this amount. Not a penny more nor a penny less."

Unknown to us, when the money ran low, Peter offered a piece of the group to anyone who provided services that he was no longer willing or able to pay for. Photographers, managers and booking agents were all given a percentage of our contract. We had a good product, but Columbia Records realized there wasn't enough left for them to make a decent profit. They released the record spending minimal funds promoting it.

Simultaneously, there was a power change at the top executive levels of Columbia. The people who were interested in us were out, and Clive Davis took over. He always claimed he liked the sound and material of The Roman Numerals, but good business practice would not allow him to promote a predecessor's product. We weren't offered a new deal. In the short time we were under contract, Columbia had moved on to new interests in hard and acid rock. In this business, timing, along with luck, and someone's personal devotion to you, have as much to do with success as talent. Four good looking guys, who sang sweet harmonies and wrote tender lyrics, missed a golden opportunity because of circumstances beyond their control.

The group landed in Cleveland unaware of these developments. We continued as planned to promote the record. Arriving at the airport on a cold winter's day, we were all shocked at what we saw. There, wiping snow off the roofs of cars, was Eddie Hilly.

I turned to my cousin Dennis. "This is where Eddie goes in the wintertime?" I said, in disbelief. I took this as a bad omen. Most people go South to Florida or some other warm climate for the season. Here, in Cleveland, Ohio, in the middle of a winter snowstorm, was Eddie Hilly.

The temperature was frigid. Since the record was to be lip-synced and our electric guitars were unamplified, Dennis and I wore gloves to spoof the situation. Elaine was unaware of our prank until the broadcast was airing. Afterwards, she was upset and told us we were acting like wise guys.

The highlight of the trip was running into Chuck Berry at the airport parking lot on our return. He recognized Johnny and remembered him from shows held almost a decade prior to our chance meeting. At these extravaganzas, dozens of Doo-Wop and Rhythmn & Blues groups like The Youngtones, performed on the bill with Chuck Berry, Little Richard, Fats Domino and other luminaries from Rock's early days.

When we returned home we learned of our fate at the record company. Johnny, over the years, had his chances. In 1958, he recorded "You I Adore" with The Youngtones, almost scoring a hit. Dick Clark offered to manage the group guaranteeing success. For such representation, he demanded 95% of all earnings for the duration of the agreement. Johnny declined. In 1962, another recording, "Shall I Tell Him You're Not Here," was climbing the charts in Rochester, Buffalo and Albany, while beginning to get play on the city's big radio stations.

At the time, one of our favorite hangouts was Dom-Joe's father's Village Pizza, located at 65 Carmine Street near Seventh Avenue South. Dom-Joe Sr. and Sonny Hap ran the place. Benny Eggs, who worked for "The Chin," sat adding up figures in his little black book. While balancing the ledger of numbers, bets and money owed the loan-sharks, he would commiserate with Dom and Sonny.

Johnny asked Dom to put the record in the jukebox. It was one of several that was routinely played. On the verge of breaking through, the record company, Big Top, went bankrupt and folded. Once again Johnny fell victim to the random tyranny of fate. Why fortune smiles on some, yet turns from others, who may posses equal or greater ability, is puzzling. It stands as one of life's curious inequities.

Now the Columbia deal wasn't living up to what it had promised to be. Maybe there was some truth to Hilly's admonition, concerning his bad luck theory, about Johnny? It was difficult to assess what wisdom lied within his alcoholic delirium.

We continued to perform, mainly in local clubs: The Bitter End, Trude Heller's and The Purple Onion being our favorite spots.

The Bitter End, located on Bleecker Street between Thompson and LaGuardia Place, was a training ground and showcase that nurtured the talents of Woody Allen, Bill Cosby, Peter, Paul and Mary, and many other young, aspiring artists. For a period of time it was owned and operated by Fred Weintraub and Roy Silver. When their partnership dissolved, Roy went to California, taking several acts with him. One of his New York groups, The Big Three, had some recognition with the recording, "Winken, Blinken, Nod." Carly Simon and her sister wrote this song when they sang as a folk duet known as The Simon Sisters. The Big Three was a trio consisting of two men and a woman. The female from that trio, Cass Elliot, traveled west with Roy, joining up with John Phillips, formerly of The Journeymen, to become a member of the highly successful group, The Mama's and Papa's. Fred remained in the city, continuing to run the club and manage his own stable of performers.

Tuesday night at the club was known as hootenanny night. There was no cover charge on this evening. Any person or group could get up on the stage and perform. The idea was to allow seasoned acts to break in new material, or new ones to audition for the management or any music business people who might be in attendance. On one such night, The Roman Numerals were introduced and offered an upbeat folk-rock composition entitled, "No Regrets." The crowd responded enthusiastically and we were encouraged to continue. We kicked it up to pure rock with another original selection, "Maze of Love." The floor manager rang up Fred, telling him, "You have to hear this group that's tearing up the place." A few minutes later Fred walked into the room. About half-way to the stage he noticed Johnny fronting the band. His reaction rang out, "Oh no, not him again." He turned on his heels, made an about face and walked out.

Franky Mouse never raised his voice. You could never tell when he was angry. He spoke softly and calmly, then did what had to be done. When you needed something, he was the one to ask.

As a teenager, not much older than thirteen, he had his family bewildered by his behavior. Every night he'd become distracted and irritable. He'd feel nauseous and sweat profusely. Sleep eluded him. He suffered terrible pains and cravings. Unable to be held down or contained, he'd flee the apartment. There was a reason he was so powerfully drawn to the street. He needed his fix. Another victim of heroin in the Italian neighborhoods, Franky Marsicovetere was hooked as a young boy.

As he grew older, and his need for money to support his habit increased, he performed services for the syndicate. He'd end up a three time felon, with a life sentence under the strict laws enacted during Governor Rockefeller's administration. A good looking man, with a pencil-thin mustache, Franky always dressed impeccably. After leaving the Village for Brooklyn, he became an operator for Crazy Joey Gallo. The reputation, the fear, the respect and all that came with it, followed.

The year was 1967. I was singing with The Roman Numerals, along with Franky's two younger brothers, Johnny and Danny, and my cousin Dennis. Rounding out the group at this time but not part of the vocal ensemble was our drummer, John Barone. Our manager was Elaine Sorel. She had been introduced to us by our vocal coach, Irma Jurist. Elaine was an artist's representative. Her clients were mainly photographers, but she was interested in branching out and getting into the music business. The lucrative opportunities and free life style of the rock and roll community, appealed to her. She was recently divorced and eager to get in on the scene.

She booked the group into the Purple Onion, on 3rd Street between 6th and MacDougal, the modern day site of The Blue Note Jazz Club. The Purple Onion was operated by two low level mafia types, or associates. They were by no means "made" men. The gig was for three weeks in December. We played four shows a night, from 8pm to 2am. When not on stage, we were confined to the basement. The owners didn't want us mingling with the patrons or the cocktail waitresses, who were dressed in bunny costumes. We were lucky to get free sodas to quench our thirst.

The engagement was stressful. We all had day jobs and other

responsibilities. I lost twenty pounds over the three week period. Getting little sleep, if any, and rising at six thirty to catch the train to Brooklyn, where I was teaching at J.H.S. 33, was exhausting.

The challenges of an inner city school were daunting. Riding the D train to the border of Williamsburg and Bedford-Stuyvesant gave a false serenity that provided no indication to the turmoil lying ahead. I embraced the emergence of the subway from underground tunnels to the morning sunrise. Crossing the East River via the Manhattan Bridge always lifted me up.

I was hopeful, but not dependent, upon success in the music business. Such dreams can prove to be chimerical. What I enjoyed was the creativity.

Years after her initial notoriety, Darlene Love, when being questioned by the media about Phil Spector's use and abuse of artists such as she, replied, "I was a nineteen year old kid who just wanted to sing." I could identify with that. It's no surprise that most educators are frustrated singers, dancers, musicians, actors and playwrights.

After a trying day at work I would muse how a hit record could change my life. Reality immediately set in each time I entered the school building. Children routinely ran through the halls screaming, pushing and knocking one another over.

Many used obscene language when addressing each other. Hand-in-hand with the cursing they liked to "rank" or insult their friends. Family members were also targets. Mothers and fathers were particularly vulnerable to this derision.

With black pride in vogue, the sharpest put-downs alleged that one's parents were lighter in skin color than was acceptable. In the past, the taunts were focused on how black one was, "Your mother's black as sin" or "Your father's blacker than coal" were bandied about. The children's interpretation of this new self-awareness had now changed in description. These former jeers were replaced with, "Your father's whiter than rice" or "Your mother's white as snow."

The term "ranking" would evolve over the years into "sounding," "snapping," and "dissing." They could all be generally classified under the category "talking trash."

Teachers were not exempt from ridicule, suffering other indignities that were directed at them. Students had no compunction about telling the authority figures, "Go fuck yourself."

The boldest boys placed their hands up teacher's dresses while ascending the stairs. Fresh out of college, dedicated yet naïve, these young women left in tears at the end of their first brutal week on the job. Many never returned.

The Black Power and Black Is Beautiful movements had an influence on the staff as well. Teachers were dividing along racial lines. In addition to the problems the student body presented, incendiary rhetoric encouraged some to be even more troublesome. This call to self-pride gave impetus to the militant teachers who already felt they were being mistreated and disenfranchised by the bureaucracy.

The greater ills of the society's neglect of race relations were surfacing. Amid this pandemonium, the principal hid in his office. No one seemed to be able to control the situation. I accepted this disorganization as part of the malaise of the system.

Though my background could hardly be considered protective, there were things I witnessed that were unexpected.

I gave a health education lesson to a seventh grade class. Two late comers, a boy and a girl, took seats in the back of the room. He had no books but was carrying a portable record player. She wore a tight sweater and was fully developed for her age.

While writing on the blackboard, I heard music emanating from the back of the room. I turned around expecting to see this charming couple dancing in the aisle. To my surprise they were still seated. He was feeling her breasts while nibbling at her ear.

I approached them and stood hands folded waiting to be recognized. This did nothing to alter their behavior. They continued as if I wasn't there. An assistant principal happened by and removed them from the class.

In a more brazen incident, the Dean caught two eighth grade students having sexual intercourse in an empty classroom. When discovered and told they would be brought to the principal's office, the girl involved queried, "What? He want some too?"

I soon thought it wise to escape the chaos of the building. One mild, pre-winter morning, I took a sixth grade class out to the school yard to play basketball and handball. Ten minutes into the period, I noticed several students huddled around an object on the ground. They were cautiously poking it with their feet. I approached and when realizing what it was, my stomach turned. I don't believe they had any idea what was in front of them. My study minor in science left no doubt it was a fetus they were kicking around. I directed the group to play elsewhere.

The most vivid recollection of the tumult was when I had an opportunity to leave school early. Halfway down the block, I could hear the final dismissal bell ringing out. The explosion of noise and reaction to the end of the day startled the pedestrians on the street. Children were screaming and breaking chairs. Occasionally, one would be tossed out an open window. The outburst was frightening in its anarchy and volume.

Little by little, the noise would diminish as I got farther and farther away. When I turned the corner, two blocks later, approaching the subway entrance, the clamor had finally dissipated to a whimper. My only thought while descending the stairs to the train platform was that I had made it through another day.

In less than a year, tensions in the school system reached the boiling point. Rhody McCoy and Sonny Carson would take over the Ocean-Hill Brownsville District. It was the beginning of community control.

The United Federation of Teachers led by Albert Shanker authorized a city-wide shut-down and a bitter strike ensued that lasted thirty-six days.

My first year in public education proved to be a baptism of fire that questioned my commitment to, and choice of, such a demanding profession.

The vocal group was laboring under difficult working conditions at The Purple Onion. Johnny was facing his own set of problems. He had recently been married and moved to a house in Staten Island. His first child, a son, John Eugene, was born.

It was getting close to the holiday and we were told we had to work Christmas Eve. We all preferred being home with family and Johnny was under particular pressure from his wife, Donna. Her parents were coming in from St. Louis and she expected him to be there. Johnny mentioned to his brother Franky how we were being treated, and the dilemma of working on the holiday. He listened attentively, telling Johnny not to get upset. He'd come by the club, December 23rd, to catch the act.

That night Franky arrived for the eleven o'clock show. In his usual dapper manner, he was elegantly dressed, wearing a silk suit. The owners practically fell over themselves in an effort to greet him. Whether they knew him personally, or not, it was obvious they knew about him. They offered to buy him a drink. Franky refused. He placed a hundred dollar bill on the bar, saying, "The drinks are on me."

While the three engaged in small talk, the group performed on the bandstand. When the set was nearing an end, Franky turned to the owners and said, "You see those guys singing up there?" "Yeah Franky," they replied, "What about them?" "They're my brothers." Franky glanced at Johnny and gave him a nod. We all put down our electric guitars, gathering around a single microphone. There we rendered an *a capella* version of "Silent Night."

Upon finishing, we proceeded to pack up our equipment. One of the goons who ran the place was a big lumbering oaf, similar to Lurch on the Adams Family. He was pissed off and was giving Dennis very dirty and threatening looks. Dennis became apprehensive and told Franky the guy was making him nervous. Franky took the initiative by ordering Lurch to help us carry the amps out. Assuring Dennis that everything was all right, Franky promised to stick around until we cleaned out and left the premises.

In essence, we had broken the contract by walking out. Our manager was concerned there would be some form of retaliation. Franky assured her there was nothing to worry about. To be on the safe side Elaine booked a series of college dates, after the New Year, that would take us out of state. She arranged for the group's overnight stay at several locations.

After finishing a show at Springfield College, we lodged for the night at a house in Connecticut. It was bitter cold. Water had frozen on the branches of the trees, and the ice glistened in the moon filled sky. We arrived at the two story house around 2am. Johnny had driven back to New York to be with his wife and child, leaving myself, Danny, Dennis and Elaine to spend the night. The first floor was crowded with people in sleeping bags and on cots. It looked like a hostel, or what today would be a homeless shelter. Our bedrooms were upstairs. We thought if we played the acoustic guitars it would help us calm down. It's difficult to recover from the adrenaline high you get performing live on stage. Elaine came into the room urging us to put the instruments away. The people sleeping downstairs had to rise in a matter of hours. Dennis and I decided to go outside to look at the stars. Danny, exhausted from the long day and night, retired to bed.

The clear sky was brilliant with light. The porch we stood on was filled with snow that had recently fallen. A crib leaned against the wood framed house. A drift, about six inches high, rested upon it.

Dennis decided to light up a joint. We hoped to settle our nerves and relax enough to go to sleep. We smoked it down to our fingertips, laughing and recalling the highlights of the evening. Satisfied, Dennis stubbed out the roach, throwing it into the snow on top of the crib. The cold had reached our bones. We went inside, put on our pajamas and got into bed.

We quickly fell out. Sometime later, we were awakened by Elaine. She was visibly upset. Thick smoke filled the room, clouding our vision and burning our eyes. We charged down the stairs and out onto the porch. The house was on fire! Flames emanated from the crib, making their way up the front wall towards the roof. Dennis and I began throwing snow on the fire in a futile attempt to put it out. Danny kept running in and out of the kitchen to fill a bucket of water. It was so cold that the spillage turned to ice as it hit the ground. The three of us repeated this folly over and over. The other house guests looked on inquisitively. We felt like The Three Stooges at a four alarmer. Within minutes the volunteer fire department arrived on the scene. They explained that a delay of five minutes more in their arrival would have caused the house to burn down to the ground.

No one directly accused us, but we were questioned along with others as to how the fire may have started. We denied any knowledge or complicity in the matter. It took a while to realize what had occurred. Obviously, the remains of the joint we smoked, that Dennis tossed into the snow, were not fully extinguished.

By the time we figured it out, we had moved on to another location. We played a few more beer party dances and fraternity gatherings. When we finished our tour of the local colleges, we returned home to wait out the winter, in hope of a more productive spring.

In the spring of 1968, the group met Jerry Kassenets and Jeff Katz, founders of Budda Records. They already had several big hits in bubble gum music, with recordings like "Yummy Yummy, I Have Love In My Tummy." They assured us they had gone as far as they could with that genre of music and were looking to produce more quality recordings. Several new songs were composed and we joined them in the studio, to lay down the tracks.

Another promising venture was the first and only Rock & Roll Singing Orchestral Circus, which they presented at Carnegie Hall on June 7, 1968. A follow-up performance on The Ed Sullivan Show was canceled after the assassination of Robert Kennedy a few days before the extravaganza at the music hall.

The show would open with an ensemble of all the groups singing on stage together. Each group would then come on and perform their own number. Jerry and Jeff asked The Roman Numerals to close the individual group portion of the show. They wanted to get the amps and other equipment behind the curtain for the big finale. This meant we would have to go out with two unplugged guitars. In their effort to choreograph a smooth transition, they had inadvertently set up a perfect situation for us. Our forte was vocal harmonization, and we delivered a gem with Johnny's strong and haunting ballad, "Daddy, Daddy."

The song begins with queries from a young girl to her father about a world she does not understand. She begins crying while her father tries to comfort her. Naïve questions about why it rains and what are friends turn to deeper introspection about man's inhumanity and the reasons for revenge, poverty, hunger and war. At the conclusion, the girl is beseeching her father not to cry. The lyrical poem speaks for itself:

Dry your eyes,
Lift your tears,
Life is still worth living.
Hide your fear,
Don't despair,
The world is waiting for you.
Daddy, Daddy,
Why does it rain?
Daddy, Daddy,
What causes pain?
Daddy, Daddy,
What are friends?
Daddy, Daddy,
What is revenge?
She broke my heart,
I saw her cry,
When she said,
Daddy, Daddy,
What's misery?
Daddy, Daddy,

What's LSD?
Daddy, Daddy,
What's poverty?
And are all men free?
Then she said,
Daddy, Daddy,
Why is there war?
Daddy, Daddy,
What is it for?
She broke my heart,
I had to cry,
Then she said,
Dry your eyes,
Lift your tears,
Daddy, don't you cry.

The acoustics at Carnegie Hall are legendary. Our voices filled the room and you could hear a pin drop in the audience during our performance. The crowd was momentarily stunned by what they had just heard in relation to what had preceded it. They gained their composure and applauded wildly.

When we exited the stage to join the others for a choral finale, we were greeted by spontaneous expressions of recognition and congratulations. Some had descended from the raised stanchions to shake our hands. These were artists who already had hit records, but were awed by our performance. Their taste and selection in music may have been insipid, but they knew something good when they heard it.

A considerable number of disc jockeys who were in the audience approached us after the performance to say they were anxiously awaiting the release of the song, "Daddy, Daddy." Numerous producers, Artie Ripp, in particular, offered their services. We had an agreement with Kassenets and Katz, and the bottom line was that the release of the song was in their hands. It was not meant to be. Jerry and Jeff had deceived us. They were not interested in going in a new direction as we were led to believe. Instead, they kept us and our music on a shelf in order to protect the viability of their own established sound. That show stopper at Carnegie Hall was to us what Andy Warhol would later refer to as one's "fifteen minutes of fame."

My thoughts returned to the days when we first started to rehearse in Johnny's bedroom, in Brooklyn. Searching to find our sound, and adapt to a new lead singer was a slow process. Danny had stepped aside as lead in deference to his older and more experienced brother. He sometimes struggled to learn the background harmonies that for years were developed around his voice. His talent would overcome any difficulties. Johnny would encourage the group reminding us that patience was a virtue. "One day," he'd say, "the harmony will be so good and tight, that you'll cum in your pants." Sex was pleasurable. So was singing and performing before a live audience. To my mind, however, the two were on completely different levels and I never quite got the analogy. Yet, that night, and on other special occasions, I experienced the power you had when holding an audience in rapture. I understood, now, on some level what Johnny was getting at. I could envision how that feeling of power and control could be intoxicating, and how one could be captivated by its magnetism and appeal.

The curse was not in the elusiveness of success. The misfortune was that we had tasted it. It is something you never forget. When you call it to mind it is elating, followed by a deep regret and loss. It is life's missed opportunities that weigh you down. It's the what-ifs, and what-could-have-beens, that haunt you.

By the close of the decade of the 1960's, we lost contact with our manager, Elaine Sorel. Twenty years later we'd reunite. I invited her and Dennis to my apartment for dinner. It was a belated thank you for all she had done in managing and promoting The Roman Numerals. After dinner we were recalling all the fun times we had together. The two week engagement at The Griswald Hotel, in Groton, Connecticut. The bookings at Carnaby's, Trude Heller's and The Purple Onion. Our triumph at Carnegie Hall. We drank a little more wine and recalled all the photo shoots, parties and recording sessions. Relaxed and at ease, we told her how we almost burnt the house down that time we were on the college circuit. She failed to see whatever humor could be found in this after such a long passage of time.

Our reunion was brief. Recalling what we tried to accomplish years ago was now filtered through time. This gave us a sharper view that included recrimination and accusation. Elaine complained that we didn't practice hard enough and that we lacked devotion. We told her she let us down by allowing Peter Steinmann to give away most of our contract.

The good times were behind us. We tried our best but didn't win the prize. It left a bitter taste in all our mouths.

Horsing Around

(Summerfallwinterspring)

Summer

As children, my sister and I accompanied my mother to the beach. This was a long trek that seemed to a young boy to take half the day. Weetsie's favorite locations were at Middle and South Beaches on Staten Island. We would take the 7th Avenue line down to Battery Park. Next came the best part of the trip, the ferry boat ride. This brought us from the southern tip of Manhattan across the Hudson River to the borough of Richmond. Along with the view of the city's skyline, passing the Statue of Liberty was always special. Once on the Island, we would either take an elevated train or bus ride for the final leg of the journey. I preferred the train because it was an older model featuring double doors and woven straw seats that were highly varnished. Depending on the waiting time for these public transportation facilities, the passage could take upwards of two hours. I always arrived feeling like I had been on a long and arduous caravan. All this just to sit and bake in the sun didn't make sense to me. Weetsie and Carole loved to do just that, leaving me in the minority with little to say. It also was easy on mom's purse. The entire outing in traveling expenses cost slightly over two dollars.

When we visited our cousins in Flushing, Uncle Pro would load up his car and we had the chance to explore more exotic locations. One place he would take us was Coney Island. The crowds were overwhelming. Just finding enough free sand to place your blanket on was a task. The memories of Nathan's hot dogs and french fries, cotton candy on a stick and over-sized soft ice cream cones still can be vividly conjured up. The boardwalk with all its arcades and attractions sent us into a frenzy of energy and activity. How many times did we ask to go into The Fun House, or be exhilarated by the Cyclone Rollercoaster and Parachute Jump? Once, when I was twelve years old, I got stuck on this ride. I must have been up there for almost an hour before they fixed the problem. The view was amazing. The rise to the top was a slow ascent and under normal conditions the anxiety and anticipation of the drop clouded out the ability to concentrate and appreciate the surrounding landscape. This day I was a captive audience and saw the entire city from a spectacular vantage point. My enchantment ended abruptly when the ride came hurtling down to the ground. The drop was so fast and surprising that my stomach felt like it was left above while the rest of my body plunged downward. My mother always saw the potential peril in any situation and used this incident as an example to persuade me never to go on these dangerous rides again. She was from the school of philosophy that espoused the following dogmas: "Your gonna poke somebody's eye out with that thing! Stop it! You'll break your neck! The answer is no, I said no! It's broken, are you happy now?" Her fear of the world was exaggerated and I never let it stifle my sense of adventure.

Other places we found exciting were Jacob Riis State Park, Jones Beach and the Rockaways. Rockaway Beach had huge barrels connected by thick, heavy rope, forming a line or barrier from the shore out into the surf. These appeared regularly at long intervals along the shoreline. What their purpose was, I did not know. If they were designed to subdue the force of the formidable waves that constantly bombarded the beach head, they were ineffective. The breakers relentlessly thundered and roared to the shore. Once, while venturing out further than I should have, a big wave knocked me over and carried me helplessly along. I found myself with my neck caught under the huge braided ropes, being submerged with each undulation. I had swallowed salt water and struggled to free myself from what in my mind was a death grip. The encounter left a nasty burn across my throat. I ran to the safety of the beach with new respect for the power and unpredictability of the ocean.

As an older teenager, I would revisit Jones Beach and the surrounding environs many times with my neighborhood friends to go on fishing expeditions. Sharky's first car was a seven year old, 1955 Jaguar Mark VII. It was a big luxury model that resembled a Rolls Royce. It featured compartments in the back of the driver and passenger seats that pulled open like trays on an airliner. One compartment held a bar with a capacity for several bottles and glasses. The other served as a stash. Usually, there were three in number on these excursions—Shark driving, me in the passenger's seat and Shark's brother, Peter, in the back. Once in a while, Shark's girlfriend, Beth, would come along. She was quite petite but made up for any shortcomings with a great amount of chutzpah. She was overly verbal, headstrong and argumentative. Such characteristics paralleled Sharky's and they were too similar in these areas to get along well. They fought ad infinitum. She rode in the passenger's seat with myself and Peter in the back. She was rarely pensive and her nervous energy was at times irritating. She complained constantly during the entire ride, and when we were about to reach our destination, would often demand that Shark turn the car around and take her home to Forest Hills. Questioning her sanity, Shark berated her while completely dismissing her tantrums and demands. Not wanting to be left out of the altercation, Peter Shark repeatedly growled, "Throw her the fuck out."

Another jaunt involved myself, Shark, Donald and a classmate from Cardinal Hayes, Joseph Bellio. Joe lived on Catherine Street in lower Manhattan and we had become friendly during high school. The night before setting off, Shark and I met in Carmine Street Park and drank a gallon of Chianti wine. We went home at midnight and rose at three o'clock in the morning. This trip had the group traveling in Joe's car. We were headed for Scotty's in Broad Channel to rent a row boat and purchase some bait. The cool moisture coming from the water that mixed with the warmer air inland created a dense fog that was so thick, it was difficult to see more than a couple of feet in front of the car. I don't know how

Joe managed to proceed without crashing into something on the highway or off. The road and the surrounding landscape were indistinguishable. For a time, we had to stop and wait for the fog to lessen.

When we arrived, Donald's father, Tilly, met up with us. He occasionally fished at nearby locations. His presence allowed us to park free at the Floyd Bennett Airport facilities. He would show a badge and we were let in without any questions. We were never quite sure what Tilly did for a living. I shared the opinion that he was a policemen for the Port Authority. Others believed he was a New York City Fireman. Each side was comfortable with their assumptions and Donald was never asked to verify either position. To this day, it is a moot point. What we knew for sure was that he was an authority figure, evidenced by his means of identification.

After securing a spot, we unloaded the fishing gear. To avoid rowing out to the deep water where the flounder were plentiful, Bellio had brought along an outboard motor to attach to the dory. It was awkward and heavy. We took turns, two at a time, carrying the engine over a considerable distance to our destination. The events of the previous night left me in no condition to exert myself. Shark, however, under the same influences, carried the motor single-handedly, demonstrating once again his strength and stamina.

Two choices I made in relation to this situation would leave me with some regret. The first was drinking the wine on the eve of the outing. The small craft rocked and rolled with every ripple. My head was throbbing and I was nauseous from the constant motion. I had an upset stomach and the taste of wine was up to my throat. I was on the verge of vomiting. Worse, I was unable to stop the sky from spinning or to maintain my equilibrium.

The second choice was participating in this venture at this time. I was facing an economics final in Dr. Mabel Chang's class at City College and I should have been home studying this particular weekend. I enrolled in summer school with the idea of taking one or two difficult subjects with the intent of concentrating on academic areas I had little interest in. Unfortunately, every time I opened the book (Samuelson's classic text), within five minutes reading time I would develop a tremendous headache. The only fact I remembered from the entire term's lectures was the maxim of bartering guns for butter. She presented this as a basic rule that somehow encapsulated the whole scope of economic theory in a nutshell. Her choppy Chinese-accented English rendered a certain degree of humor to her proposition. Hearing it over and over just made me hungry, and I knew committing this pragmatism to memory would not be sufficient to get me through the final. When I should have had my nose to the grindstone, I was out fishing. Obviously, my activities had their priority. Singing, playing and rehearsing with the band came first. Life on the street with Sharky followed. Devotion to scholastics ran a distant third.

An upset stomach, hangover and bad sunburn were the least of the ramifications of that day. I paid a greater price for my horse play when I did poorly on my economics final and received a D as my grade in the course.

Fall

My cousin Dennis lived at 272 Bleecker Street on the corner of Morton right next to the renowned John's Pizzeria. It was a building that housed several of the Village's notable families. The Vella's, along with Vinny Vella[4] and his many siblings lived at this location. His older sister, Isabella, was a classmate of mine. She had attended the neighborhood public and parochial schools being left back during the course of her movements. Straggly black hair and a hook nose similar to Margaret Hamilton, the Wicked Witch of the West in *The Wizard of Oz*, were her prominent features. Fittingly, one Halloween she was sent to school with a silver streak in her hair and a broom. No fancy expensive costume was required.

The youngest in the family was Nicky. I was four to five years his senior. Most of the Vella's were left back at least one grade and it was difficult to assess exactly how old they were. At sixteen, I was returning home for an eleven o'clock curfew. Passing 272 Bleecker, I would witness Nicky screaming up to the fifth floor

---

[4] See NY Metro's "Hey Vinny" for a portrait of this colorful character.

window. He was addressing his mother. "Hey, you stupid bitch. Throw down some fucking money. I want to go to Coney Island."

His tirade would cause her to acquiesce to his demands. She would toss down several dollars for his evening's entertainment.

I was heading home while twelve year old Nicky was taking the subway to the arcades along the famed boardwalk.

There were other Vella's who were older brothers and sisters that were not part of my social circle. I knew nothing of their lives.

Vinny's best friend and side kick, Eugene Delgado, also lived here. It was the domicile of my friend and classmate, Michael (Black/Beulah) Sciarillo. In apartment 23 were my cousins, the Genoveses, Dennis and his younger brothers Robert and Andrew. Dennis and I spent many hours there singing, playing guitars and recording on a reel-to-reel tape recorder. Robert, Dennis' middle brother was old enough to be hanging out with his friends. Andrew, the youngest, was more impressed by what we were doing. He later became a musician, opting to play the drums. Several incidents involving him were memorable. One time our manager, Elaine Sorel, visited Dennis with her daughter Louise. She and Andrew were similar in age and were left to their own devices. Andrew spent the afternoon chasing Louise around the apartment trying to put his hand up her dress. Another occasion found us rushing Andrew to the hospital. In a laughing fit, a jaw-breaker he was sucking on moved up his windpipe and lodged itself in his nostril. Such calamities were the norm at 272 Bleecker Street.

Once, Dennis and I arrived there late at night whacked on weed. Dennis decided to declare a war of the roaches and we went into the early morning fumigating the apartment with insecticide from a spray gun. The rest of the family managed to sleep soundly throughout this assault.

One Saturday morning found my cousin Dennis and I traveling north on the subway to Central Park. Danny Mouse had become a decent horseback rider after several years of involvement. His usual practice was to go to riding academies and stables in Forest Hills, accompanied by his friends, Dapper Dan, Ziggy and his older brother, Johnny. Danny had never been on the trails in Central Park and Dennis and I felt it would be a good opportunity to be introduced to the sport and have some fun. We secured three horses from the Claremont Riding Academy at 89th Street off Central Park West. This was the oldest established business furnishing horses to the bridal paths designed for the park by its creators, Olmsted and Vaux. This facility was set into operation within five years of the park's opening in the late 1800's. In an effort not to burden Danny with a nag, or thwart his experience, Dennis and I assured the stable hand that we were all seasoned riders. Accordingly, he obliged us by delivering two steeds that were equal to the fine animal Danny had selected. Being neophytes, Dennis and I did not have a clue as to the rudimentary skills of equestrian management. Our misrepresentation became immediately apparent when the horses were brought out and we tried to mount them. The beasts kept circling around as we clumsily tried to get our feet in the stirrups. When we did manage to climb on their backs, it would only be a matter of moments before we slipped off and fell to the ground. Several failed attempts led the stable boy to approach and question our ability to handle our charges. We insisted that everything was fine and under control. The horses, sensing our tentativeness and lack of direction, knew better. We had not yet realized we would soon be at their mercy!

Crossing the traffic on Central Park West, we entered the park. Danny led the way, while Dennis and I followed behind, side by side. We had been on the trail only a short time when Dennis lit up a cigarette, then quickly decided to put it out. His horse was already getting feisty and he realized he needed both hands on the reins. Foolishly, he attempted to extinguish the butt on the rear of the saddle. Something went awry. Either sparks shot off onto the horse's skin or Dennis inadvertently stubbed the Winston into its rump, believing it to be the leather saddle. Whatever the case, the horse suddenly bolted forward into a full gallop. My horse followed suit. We were racing along unable to slow down the stampede. Unaware of the events leading to this debacle, Danny looked bewildered as we sped past him. To my surprise, the horse I was on left the path and began riding on the sidewalk, running parallel to an eight foot cyclone fence that encircled the Reservoir. Looking ahead, I saw the low hung branches of an imposing oak tree in our path. The horse would take no direction from me and continued straight toward this obstruction. The limbs were just the right height to knock me off my ride and possible cause further injury. The last ten feet were rapidly approaching and I had to make a quick decision. In a drastic maneuver, I dove off the horse just in time to avoid being decapitated.

Dennis's dismount was also not of his own choosing. His horse had thrown him and would not allow his re-mounting. I climbed atop my steed believing I could continue to ride. I had paid $30 for the hour, and so far, had not gotten my money's worth. My horse would have none of it and followed Dennis's back to the stable. My cousin was now following on foot.

When we came to Central Park West, both horses crossed against traffic. Cars and taxis came to a screeching halt to allow the animals their way. They were eager and determined to get back to the stable, especially the horse Dennis had used as an ashtray.

We had been out less than fifteen minutes and our ride was over. We sat on the curb and waited the rest of the hour for Danny to return. Dennis and I accepted this episode as our first, and perhaps only, equestrian experience. We rode the train back to the Village. Danny went home to Brooklyn, to be with Sandy and their daughters, Robin, Jodi and Karen.

Winter

The Roman Numerals spent much of the winter of 1967-68 rehearsing several nights a week in a studio on 44th Street and 8th Avenue. Dennis and I would stop off at the Shamrock Bar for a roast beef sandwich before rendezvousing with Johnny and Danny to complete the quartet. Our financial backer had made all the arrangements and we were to polish our material and work on new compositions. We usually spent three hours from seven to ten in the evening. We were putting together an anti-war Christmas ballad titled, "Hard to Get Love," which was Johnny's latest effort.[5] We were stuck for a transition in and out of the channel, or middle break. Suddenly, the Bob Gibson carol, "Virgin Mary Had One Son," came to mind. We took the interweaving harmonies we had worked up for that song and utilized them to embellish and complete our new creation.

The studio was an aging and dilapidated walkup with several rooms on each floor. An older gentleman named Lou, who let everyone know he was gay, ran the place. He was good natured, easy to talk with and quick with a joke. He liked the group and seemed always happy to see us, smiling whenever we passed his reception area entering or exiting the building.

It was a Friday night and we were all looking forward to a break in the routine with time to spare. On our way out we bade Lou goodnight, inquiring what he might be doing the next couple of days. His reply was always the same, "Boys, I'm gonna be fucking and sucking all weekend long. I hope you have a hell of a time, too." Fortunately, this was well before the AIDS crisis hit, and Lou had no reason to be concerned about his activities.

Saturday morning, my cousin Dennis and I made our way to the Brill Building on 48th Street and Broadway. We were looking for a man named Andy Pace. We had previously engaged him in the Village to give us a guitar lesson. We were anxious to learn styles of finger picking and he assured us he could demonstrate and teach such techniques. The location was familiar to us. Over the years, we had met some interesting people there. At one time or another, we had business with Doc Pomus and Mort Shuman, Johnny Beanstalk, Phil Spector and Artie Ripp.

We entered a small office where our musical instructor was located. Dennis and I handed over the $20 fee we had agreed upon during our first encounter with Mr. Pace. He was a husky black man with huge hands. As soon as he picked up a guitar, doubt set in. His stubby fingers crushed the strings and he could not manage to fit them within the frets to organize a cord. If he had laid his thumb

---

[5]   For complete lyrics to this song, please refer to Appendix C.

across the board and barred the fret, in the manner of playing that Richie Havens had popularized, I would have been encouraged. In this way, he could have strummed the instrument while producing something musical instead of merely mauling the neck of his Stratocaster. To our dismay, he never got that far. He insisted on giving a lecture on how to dress and present ourselves on stage. He came across as a hold over from the Doo-Wop era; someone who was more interested in teaching fancy dance steps and stage choreography to compliment our vocalizing. He missed, or failed to grasp, the momentous changes brought about by The Beatles and the rest of the British invasion. In his own words, he was going to show us how to put together "a 'fessional ack." It did not take long to realize he could not differentiate "Travis" picking from picking cotton. The fact that he brandished a Fender should have alerted us to the possibility that folk music was not his bag. Our money had been squandered and we left frustrated and disappointed. Another skill we would have to learn by ourselves. Consequently, we would spend hours listening to Peter, Paul and Mary albums. By trial and error, and with a degree of musical acumen, we eventually emerged with our interpretation of these picking styles.

After our let down with Andy, we ran into a fellow on the elevator who was overbearingly verbose, demonstrating no inhibitions in addressing strangers and promoting himself and his concerns. His name was Nicky and he was about our age. We had met him once before and knew of his desire to break into the music business. As we exited the building onto Broadway, he kept us captivated for some time by his harangue. Exactly what he did and what his talents were never came across. He did not sing or play an instrument. His capacity to talk led us to believe he was interested in representing artists as an agent or manager. After being in his presence more than once, we came to the conclusion that his true skill was in peppering his conversational speech with every conceivable declension of the word fuck. He used it as a noun, adjective, verb and adverb. This occurred strictly by chance, since parsing a sentence was beyond his ken. Customary monologue from Nicky sounded like this: "I met this fucking guy Joe. I told this fuck not to fucking fuck with me, or

I'd fucking kick the fuck out of him. Who the fuck does he fucking think he's fucking with? The son of a fucking bitch. Fuck, fucking him." First impressions are lasting. Did he actually think this offensive approach was a way to adequately present himself or represent others? True to the intent of a nickname, we would use his own verbalizations to identify and characterize him in the future. Whenever we referred to him amongst ourselves or to explain what he was about to those who had never met him, we simply called him "Fucking Nicky."

Spring

I often spent time with my friends from 13 Carmine Street. My classmate Richard Palandrani, his cousin Ricardo Pecora and the Miguez brothers, Fernando and John. John owned and operated a business in which he sold and fixed copying machines. It was a fledgling concern that he maintained for several years before joining his father-in-law's plumbing outfit. One of his employees in the Xerox enterprise was a Cuban émigré named Rubén Rebasa. An arrangement was made to meet him in Astoria, Queens to look at a sports coupe he was interested in buying. Rubén had difficulty with the language, speaking English with a heavy Spanish accent. He was a tall, prematurely bald man who was soft-spoken and backward in manner. He was a decent fellow, but somewhat of a mama's boy. Although John was protective of him, he easily fell into the role of a lackey and was treated accordingly. His serious attempts to grasp his adopted language and culture came off as funny, and his effeminate nature did nothing to alter our perception of him or the amusement it generated.

The group proceeded by automobile to the prearranged location. As was customary on such excursions, we rolled a handful of joints and set off to see where the day would take us. Upon reaching our destination, we noticed Rubén was already on the site. He paced back and forth, anxiously awaiting our arrival.

The foreign car dealership was impressive. It featured all the roadsters that were in vogue. Rubén entered into a conversation with John. He manifested a certain quality of sorrow and dolor that often left him on the verge of tears. He was by nature a whiner and complainer, bordering on nervous hysteria. John, playing the role of the older, wiser, more sophisticated big brother, made efforts to calm Rubén down, imploring him to concentrate on the task at hand. The rest of the group, feeling good from the ride, found this all amusing. Rubén was an easy mark. If we paid attention, our amusement could easily turn into hilarity. In our condition it was a reasonable segue.

The salesman approached to discern what Rubén was seeking. He exchanged pleasantries and offered a routine sales pitch. The two then got into an MG Spider, Rubén in the driver's seat. He could barely fit his gangly body into the cramped compartment. The oversized steering wheel reached his chin. His head pressed against the hard-top roof. In the passenger's seat, the salesmen with clipboard in hand, directed Rubén to turn the ignition on and go for a spin. The mechanics of the stick-shift automobile bewildered him. The car darted forward and back a few feet in each direction in his futile attempt to test drive it. The salesman tried to maintain his composure during Rubén's desperate and clumsy efforts to engaged the clutch.

A near fender-bender with a fire hydrant located on the lot ended the fiasco. The salesman turned to Rubén with a puzzled look on his face. Disheveled and annoyed, he questioned Rubén's ability to drive a standard machine. Rubén realized the man's patience had run out. He brought the car to a halt, twisted his body and poked his head out the window. Frightened, confused and exasperated, he turned to John, his boss and friend, and bemoaned, "What do I do now, Yonny?!"

The rest of the group laughed so hard we practically rolled to the ground and into the traffic on the busy thoroughfare. John spent some time consoling Rubén, then sent him back to the subway he came on. The rest of us returned to the car. Still laughing, we lit up a joint and traveled back to the Village.

Out of this World

Tripping the Light Fantastic

The decade of the 1960's, especially after the arrival and prominence of The Beatles and Bob Dylan, was a journey in drug experimentation.

Our American history, particularly in the twentieth century, is observed and catalogued by decades. These ten year spans identify the events and people within. The eras of The Great War in the teens, The Roaring Twenties, The Depression of the thirties, The Second World War of the forties, the prosperity and complacency of the fifties, all had their unique characteristics.

Sex and drugs were always around. When mixed with Rock & Roll, this combination became explosive and would dominate the youth growing up in the sixties. Coming off the conservatism of the previous decade, the sexual and drug revolutions would turn the culture upside down.

The Village was always a hotbed for radical ideas, the avant guard, an embracing of alternative lifestyles and flexibility with experimentation in all areas. I'm certain what we were experiencing was being played out in big cities and small towns all across the country. I'm also convinced we didn't miss out on any of it.

At one time or another my friends and I smoked pot, hashish and opium. Took speed and cocaine. Popped amphetamines to get up and barbiturates to come down. Ate peyote, (psychedelic mushrooms) and brownies filled with hash or marijuana. We laced our joints with PCP (angel dust) and other drugs I cannot remember the names of. Liquor, wine and beer washed all of this down.

Our curiosity turned to LSD and in 1965 I asked my friend and colleague, Bob Morgenstern, who attended City College with me, to supply us with a couple of cubes. I knew he had tried it, and there were times he came to classes under its influence. He followed through by selling me three capsules of the drug.

Danny Mouse and I decided to visit Ziggy at the Marlton Hotel on 8th Street. We picked up a bottle of Mateus and headed over. I distributed the capsules, but Danny had a better idea. He suggested emptying their contents into the wine. We began passing the bottle around. Drinking, talking and playing guitars, we realized almost an hour had passed. The guys started to complain. Ziggy said, "What did your friend give you?" Danny chimed in with, "We were beat. Your friend ripped us off." We were all resigned to the fact that something went wrong when suddenly the three of us were rolling on the floor, hysterical with laughter.

All of a sudden everything looked different. Light and color were dancing around giving us a kaleidoscopic view of the world. We'd entered a new dimension, like Alice in Wonderland. It took time to compose ourselves and risk venturing onto the street to take in the sights and sounds of Greenwich Village night life.

Everything people did became exaggerated. A large woman, peeling and eating a banana, was transformed into a gorilla feeding itself at the zoo. The drug was an extreme up which intensified all the senses. We found amusement everywhere, and were exhausting ourselves by sheer observation and hilarity. Watching things so closely turned into an inner paranoia, exposing our own behavior to the scrutiny of others. We became suspicious and vulnerable. The mass of humanity became overwhelming. We retreated back upstairs to Ziggy's room to re-focus and calm down. As the expression goes, we were flying.

We amused one another by playing the guitars and singing. An undeterminable amount of time passed. We settled down believing the "trip" was over. Again, out of nowhere, we found ourselves laughing hysterically. We decided to walk through Washington Square Park.

This area was always crowded on a weekend night, offering a huge venue for interaction. Viewed under the influence of the drug, peoples' behavior became caricatured. All their actions and movements appeared funny and offbeat. When we realized our conduct was becoming stranger than the people we were watching, we'd hurry back to the hotel. The drug began to worry us. Every time we'd settle down believing it was over, we'd end up laughing uncontrollably. We were right back in the power of the acid. We feared this pattern would continue without end. Would we forever drift in and out of this high? People who were more experienced with LSD claimed that once you took it, you were prone to get flashbacks for years to come. We had entered new territory and could not reverse its consequences.

The reality of the night moving into a new day, with its own set of demands, took precedence, forcing the three of us to head home. We parted on the corner of 8th Street and University Place. That night and the next, I lay in bed listening to my heartbeat. Sleep was impossible. The laughing fits ended. No more brilliant colors and dazzling light shows. What remained was an unnatural amount of energy for the next couple of days. My friend Bob hadn't beat us after all. This was a wonderfully mysterious adventure I'd experiment with several times before encountering the dark side of the drug.

I shared several interests with my brother-in-law, Roddy, born Corrado DiStefano. We both sang, played guitar and composed songs. Enjoying these creative activities, we'd engage in them whenever the occasion arose. Limited time was available to pursue these regards because of our difference in lifestyles. I was recently married to his sister, Angela, while Roddy was living, and attending college, in upstate New York. His search for identity and contentment would eventually lead him to California. When he went out west, I loaned him a hand made Michael Gurian six string steel guitar to replace the old, inferior instrument he had outgrown. A good friend, David Noferi, gave it to me. Within a year, Roddy's apartment was broken into. The guitar was stolen and never recovered. I still wish it was part of my collection.

Roddy would visit whenever possible. These trips home became less frequent after he met someone and started a serious relationship. A decade long courtship and living arrangement resulted in a marriage that lasted a year.

Before embarking on that Odyssey, he, Angela and I, dropped acid and went to the Pet & Farm Animal Show at the Coliseum in Columbus Circle. Why we went there escapes me, but it was a memorable outing.

Overtaken and compelled by the power of the drug, the three of us climbed over the fences separating the animals from the rest. Our unbridled enthusiasm found us mixing with them in the dirt and slop. This frolicking ended up in the turkey house, with the three of us chasing the birds around. Security personnel requested we leave, or be escorted out. Before departing, we managed to purchase three items: a turtle, a snake and a small lizard!

We returned to my wife's parent's place at 11 Carmine Street. Angela and Roddy lived here along with their cousin, Kathleen Pope. Elizabeth Kilgallen, girlfriend of Johnny Howard, also resided there. Nocetti owned and operated a hardware store on street level and was also the building's landlord.

Angela's parents, Anna and Sam (whose real name was Rosario) lived on the third floor. Clara, Anna's mother, lived below. Sam frequently retold the story of how Clara was instructed in English to address a potential employer in the hope of securing a position at the factory where several family members worked. Having no facility, at the time, in her adopted language, she painstakingly learned her verbal presentation by repetition.

After hours of preparation and rehearsal, she presented herself for an interview. The foreman greeted her saying, "Hello Madam, what can I do for you?" As trained, she replied to her prospective boss, "Good morning, Mr. Jackass, you got a job for me you son of a bitch?" She smiled, beseechingly, awaiting some positive affirmation. The indication that things had not gone well was immediately apparent. Regardless of the communication barrier, she could see the look of anger and embarrassment on the man's face. Stunned and confused, she left the factory. The joke was played, the job was lost.

Clara was visiting when the three of us arrived. We were all still visibly in an altered state. Wide eyed, and grinning from ear to ear, we emptied the contents of our afternoon safari on their living room floor. My mother-in-law, Anna, was suspicious the minute we came through the door. She knew something was up but couldn't put her finger on exactly what it was. Sammy, a good-natured man, immediately took our side. He defended us and commiserated with our antics. The laughter was becoming uncontrollable. Angela was hysterical and I kept urging her to gain control. I noticed the look of surprise and panic growing on her mother's face. The more I tried to calm them down, the more Angela and Roddy became oblivious to anything other than the trip they were on.

Amid all this merriment, the turtle, snake and lizard had branched out from the living room and were exploring the apartment. Meanwhile, I was trying to quiet down Angela, Sammy was trying to smooth things over with Anna, who by now was jumping up and down in a fit of nervous agitation.

Grandma Clara, visibly upset, stood on the side watching this drama unfold. She was dressed in her everyday mourning attire. This consisted of black shoes, black stockings and a black dress. On cool evenings she would add a black shawl. A black lace net over her hair completed the wardrobe whenever she attended church. In appearance, it seemed she was always coming from or going to a Sicilian funeral.

Amid such disorder, Clara often became exasperated, and as a reaction to the changing fortunes of life, would routinely threaten to "put her head in the oven." This was basically a ploy for attention and an idle menace, since she never actually followed through.

Her laments, along with Roddy crawling around on his hands and knees looking for the critters, put the finishing touches to this Theater of the Absurd. The best way to describe what was going on would be to visualize Marlin Perkins, on acid, hosting and episode of "Mutual of Omaha's Wild Kingdom."

I can't recall how we talked our way out of that situation. I'm sure Angela's parents were just happy we eventually came to our senses and returned to normal behavior.

One spring afternoon, Angela and I went to the Bronx Botanical Gardens. Bobby Perazzo, a good friend of Roddy's, who would become a close friend of mine, joined us. This friendship included being invited to his wedding. He married his girlfriend, Angel, in her parish church and held a big party in Brooklyn. Everyone danced, drank and had a wonderful time. After the celebration ended, Angela and I rode the train back to Manhattan. It was an afternoon affair, and there was still a few hours of light left. We exited the subway on Broadway and Lafayette and walked the eight blocks west on Houston to MacDougal Street. I happened to glance back, and to my surprise, saw the bride a block behind. She was in her bridal gown and was carrying the sack she had stuffed with all the envelopes and cards that were collected at the reception. Each time she stepped onto a curb, she would lift her veil and dress, to avoid soiling them. As we neared the apartment, I noticed she was still following. When we came to the building, Angela suggested we talk for a few minutes on the sidewalk before entering. Angel appeared from around the corner and joined in our conversation. She made small talk, discussing the happy event and what a good time all the participants had. This dialogue went on for about twenty minutes. It seemed that she had no pressing engagements, so Angela invited her in for a cup of coffee.

The ladies and I sat in the living room for hours talking about nothing in particular. Around midnight, I said good night, and retired to the bedroom. When I woke in the morning, I found Angel asleep on the couch, still wearing her nuptial attire. The sofa was a six foot long masterpiece of furniture that we purchased from Carderelli and Sons. The red velvet fabric on the couch, in contrast to the white satin and lace of the gown, presented a vivid and lasting picture. Why she spent her matrimonial night in our apartment was perplexing. She never offered an explanation and we never asked for one.

Bobby later explained they had agreed beforehand that the union would not work and they would split amicably. Because everything was paid for, and in order not to disappoint anyone, they went through with the ceremony and its accompanying festivities. They divided the money and received an annulment which the church was willing to grant for the sum of $600.

Strange things happen under the influence of drugs, but this bizarre event was virtually substance free. Reality can be stranger than fiction. In retrospect, the episode resonates with the makings of an hallucinatory dream. The real psychedelics, however, turned frightening on our visit to the conservatory. This experiment with LSD would be my last.

After the drug took effect we jumped on a trolley car to ride around the park. On a whim, I jumped off the tram while it was in motion. I tripped and fell to the ground. Rolling over, in what appeared to be slow motion, I rose to my feet. Running a few paces, I leapt back into the moving car, landing in the same seat I had abruptly left. All this was accomplished in one smooth continuous flow. Bobby looked at me in astonishment. "How did you do that?" he asked, adding, "Without breaking your neck?" I could offer no explanation. I always possessed good balance but this feat was acrobatic.

As I walked through the crowds, my body took on an ethereal quality. I was floating on a cloud. A spectral spirit among mortals. Weaving in and out of the open spaces between people, I felt as light as a feather, deftly avoiding any contact. It seemed I wasn't occupying the space I was in.

All my senses were reaching a fever pitch. The gardens, full of flowers, bushes and trees, depicted a wonderland of flora. I paused to look at the trees and was amazed to see hundreds of dew lines connecting their branches. I became mesmerized. Further observation convinced me these lines linked every tree that was visible. To my chagrin, no one else saw this phenomenon. Was it my heightened sense of awareness or an illusion? When you're high on LSD you believe the reality of what you're experiencing. Because of the mind altering properties of the drug, you never know for sure. Anything can grab your attention and engross you for much longer than your interest would normally require.

There was too much stimulation outdoors so I went into a bathroom to relieve myself and escape the titillation. I began urinating and immediately became engrossed in my own bodily function. I expelled what seemed to be an inordinate amount of fluid. My attention then focused on each droplet, which to my mind, was moving in slow motion. From the head of my penis down to the drain in the urinal, each beads fall was an individual journey and adventure. A fascinating flow of life. I became uneasy and turned to catch someone watching me. In truth, I was the voyeur. My witness was more precisely a meta-voyeur; a person who watches a person who is watching. I was uncomfortable at being observed in such a situation. I washed, and quickly exited the men's room.

The clouds had given way to a brilliant sun. While strolling under its radiance I began to lose my equilibrium. My homeostasis thrown off I felt anxious, nauseous and irritable. Energy was flooding through my body which seemed too forceful to contain. Each cell in me felt like it was ready to explode and become part of the sun. I was rapidly losing control and drifting away. My heart was racing. My breathing labored. I was in a cold sweat with the aura of flashing lights adding to the disorientation. I lied down on the grass and prayed it would go away. This is what people referred to as a bad trip. Buildings falling on them, or being swallowed up by a couch, or eaten by bugs. It was now happening to me. Terrible things were not coming from the outside, but from within my own body.

I held on and eventually the crisis past. I didn't explode. I didn't become part of the sun. I made it back. My flirtation with LSD was over.

The Outer Twilight Zone Limits

My attitude towards religion was framed by the experiences I encountered. Though I lost the fervor and confidence in those who professed its dogma, I remained a spiritual minded person. I stopped attending mass and going to confession during my sophomore year at Cardinal Hayes.

After my friends and I inadvertently set a parked truck on fire, I found myself relating this incident in the confessional before attending an Easter novena. The priest responded, "*Paesan*, you've got to take it easy." I became upset at his declaration. How did he know I was a *paesan*? How did he know I was Italian? There were plenty of Irish kids in the school, mixed with some Puerto Rican and African Americans. I felt awkward and vulnerable. Not only because my identity may have been compromised, but also the telling of intimate and personal details of my life to a third party was becoming embarrassing and unpalatable. At this point I began drifting away from the church. It was during this period that the first of three eerie incidences occurred. They say things happen in threes. It is a recognizable number in our civilization and culture: The Trinity, The Three Wise Men, Columbus's Three Ships, The Three Musketeers, et cetera. These events happened over a ten-year period. A relatively short time in the span of a lifetime. They leave room for interpretation and explanation. To quote the Bard, "There are more things in heaven and earth than are dreamt of in your philosophy."

The first occurred in 1960, when I was fifteen and working as a delivery boy for a dry cleaning store. The shop, located on MacDougal Street between Bleecker and Houston, was owned and operated by Nat and Mary Paladino. Nat ran the business and his wife did the tailoring.

It was a simple assignment. Deliver the clothes to the proper address and collect the money due. Rather routine, until the day I was sent to a townhouse on 9th Street between 5th and 6th Avenues.

The brownstone was a typical building of its kind. Several steps off the sidewalk led to a big wooden front door. There were quite a few structures of similar architectural design on the block, and I assumed people of means lived here. It always interested me to observe how other people lived. Especially the middle and upper classes, since I had limited exposure to their lifestyles in my early youth.

When I entered the apartment on the second level, I was immediately taken over by a feeling I could not explain. I sensed, in every way, that I knew this place and had been here before. Positive this was not the case, I couldn't let go of this perception of recognition. Nothing came as a surprise. Not the layout of the rooms or the warm feelings I had being in them. More than at ease, I felt at home. How could I enter a strange place that was so familiar to me? A different consciousness had taken over in this environment. I never again had the feeling of completely knowing something I was experiencing for the first time.

Was it a longing for things I did not possess, or an obscure psychic memory of things that once were part of my world? I could only conjecture that I may have lived there in a previous life. Beyond a satisfactory explanation, it left me curious and bewildered.

I returned to the shop and waited for my next delivery. I kept this to myself, not knowing what to make of it. It turned out to be a singular event. But then again, isn't everything in life?

I was to be married in December 1968. In August of that year, we went for a blood test in order to procure a license. My future wife, Angela, brought me to her doctor, a woman, for the sample. I stood, watching a full vial of fluid being extracted from my arm. Everything was fine until she pulled the needle out. After realizing how much of my blood was in that tube I went into shock.

My macho bravado, which kept me from lying down or turning my head, had undone me. I began to drift away knowing I would soon pass out. I actually felt my spirit leave my body. It hovered over the room watching this drama play out. It was surrealistic and the farce was just beginning.

By now the doctor had lain me down on a table and was frantically trying to revive me. She was running around the room searching for something to administer. She located a box of smelling salts. She broke one open and placed it under my nose. I didn't respond. She tried again to no avail. I was white as a ghost and she wasn't far behind. As her attempts continued to fail she became more desperate and ashen. I watched from above in a confused state of anxiety and amusement. I could understand her dilemma.

I came for a simple blood test and dropped dead in her office. The procedure was successful but the patient didn't make it.

This out of body experience was unique but frightening. Nothing like this had ever happened to me before. I felt my spirit was attached to my body by a string that kept moving farther away. As it did, the string was getting thinner and thinner. Like a balloon that escapes a child's hand and floats away into the sky, I knew, in whatever consciousness I had, if that string broke, it was over. I'd be gone without any way of coming back.

Everything was playing out at a rapid pace. The doctor desperately trying to revive me, my existence gradually slipping away, while my spirit hovered over the room watching it all.

At the last second before the string was about to break, I snapped out of it and came to. Usually, coming out of a fainting spell proceeds gradually. You start hearing voices then open your eyes to images, which are blurry at first, that eventually come into focus. My recovery was like running into a wall. One moment I was gone, and the next I was fully cognizant. It happened that fast.

I felt compassion for the doctor. I wasn't her patient. This would be the first and only time I would use her services. She was badly shaken. Fortunately, things had turned out well. I had faced the *Paraclyte of Corbaca*, the Angel of Death, and walked away. From that day on I lie down and look away when someone takes my blood.

Six months later the last of this trilogy of uncanny happenings took place. I was married in December 1968, and the apartment we rented on MacDougal and Houston Streets was to be available the previous August. When the time arrived, Phil, the tenant who was to move out, asked us for a two-week extension. Since we weren't moving in until the end of the year, there was no problem. When he cleared out he left us a new light fixture in the entrance foyer as a present and a thank you for our kindness and consideration. We had been in his company twice. When he left we offered our best wishes on his retirement and relocation. Angela and I settled into the apartment in early December.

A cold stormy night in February 1969 is still haunting. The rain was heavy and non-stop as it beat against the windows. The wind was howling and we were happy to be at home watching television in our warm apartment. We both retired to bed around midnight. At 2am, we were awakened by the ringing of the doorbell. Curious as to who would be visiting at such an hour, I got out of bed and peered through the peephole. No one was there. I returned to bed. The bell rang again. I ignored the sound believing it to be a prankster. A few minutes later, there was a knocking at the door. I checked the peephole again and saw nothing. Not satisfied, I opened the door and noticed the hallway was empty. Anyone coming out of the pouring rain to knock on our door would have left a puddle of water. The floor was completely dry.

I decided to look out the kitchen window onto the street. Under normal circumstances I could see anyone who was standing at the doorway to the front entrance. Angela had followed me and anxiously asked, "What do you see out there?" It was dark with poor visibility. My gut feeling was that it was the man who previously lived here. Why I thought I saw him, a man I barely knew, standing in the rain on this dreadful evening, I can't explain. She asked once more, "Who's out there?" I hesitatingly answered, "I think it's that guy Phil, the former tenant." I opened the apartment door and looked down the hallway to the front entrance. There was no one there.

Angela and I were both on edge. We heard the door bell ring and the knock on the door, yet no one could be found. Why I believed it was Phil remained unclear. I had only met the man twice. Identifying him under such conditions was dubious. I just had this premonition that it was he. It took us awhile to settle down and return to bed.

The incident was put out of mind. The following weekend the weather was unseasonably warm. The sun shone brightly and we were awakened to hear our neighbors in animated conversation outside our kitchen window. We went outside to see what all the fuss was about. They asked us if we heard the news. To our astonishment they explained how the man who used to live in our apartment drowned in a boating accident the previous weekend. The night I thought I saw him, he tragically died.

Why did he return? What was he looking for in the apartment? Was there some kind of unfinished business here? Maybe he was just coming back to the last place that was peaceful and secure. These and many other questions lingered. I thought, perhaps, he had hidden money, jewels or other valuables that he somehow forgot. I searched every closet and loose floorboard for hidden compartments.

I never found anything. When we moved from the apartment several years later, Angela left the light fixture behind. Phil's apparition, and the uncanny feeling that accompanied it, still lingered. Why he returned remains a mystery. I will never forget him standing out there in the rain. Dead men do tell tales.

A Night at The Plaza

I count Richard Palandrani among my oldest friends. We went through elementary school together, many years in the same class, and have maintained a life long friendship.

As a normal progression we went to competing high schools and chose different careers. While pursuing separate interests, we always managed to come together and enjoy life, especially during the turbulent period of adolescence and early adulthood. We had many fun times. Whether driving to Wetsons in Rockaway for a meal of hamburgers, fries and a shake, that was bought for less than a dollar, or going up to Peekskill with the whole gang, it was always an adventure.

The gang included Richie, his cousin Ricardo Pecora, and their friends, the Miguez brothers, Fernando and John. They all lived in the same building on Carmine Street between Bleecker and 6th Avenue, across from Father Demo Square.

We'd meet by the pool where Richie was a lifeguard. He worked there for many years while pursuing his dream to become an architect. The head lifeguard, Bob Daly, became a friend and mentor to us all. A self-taught rabble-rouser, he inspired us to question everything presented to us. Most importantly, he encouraged us to read good books, and to respect the written word. He introduced us to books such as "The Manchurian Candidate" and authors like Ayn Rand. We consumed "Atlas Shrugged" and "The Fountainhead." The seeds of Richie's profession started with Howard Roark.

Setting off from the Village in someone's old car, the ride to Peekskill was both entertaining and dangerous. We enjoyed playing the radio while traveling to the country. Invariably, due to a preliminary round of smoking cannabis, with frequent toking along the way, Fernando, or Nando as we called him, often found himself on the wrong side of the road. Going up a sharply curved mountain into the on coming lane, made us highly vulnerable to a crash. With our hearts pounding like parakeets, we'd scream furiously, until Nando veered out of the way just in time to avoid a collision. Despite our recklessness, we always managed to get there unharmed.

The Palandranis and Pecoras owned a small house on a plot that was directly off the thoroughfare. Dirt roads were common then and we could play for long periods of time before a single automobile passed by. Not far away was a quarry where we often climbed rocks and swam in the pond.

Richie and Cardo's grandmother, Nonna, was the matriarch of the family. She smoked those De Nobali cigars, the one's we called guinea stinkers. She'd drink wine and tell stories and offer advice. In her later years she tended to drift off, but was always delightful to be around.

As I was included in things they did, I'd reciprocate by inviting them to special get-togethers. We all joined together in a raucous party marking the end of the most tumultuous decade of our lives. This decade included the tragic deaths of Jimi Hendrix, Janis Joplin, Brian Jones and Jim Morrison. It beheld the assassinations of JFK, Martin Luther King and Robert Kennedy. It witnessed the destructiveness of the Vietnam War, the senseless deaths at the Rolling Stone's Altamont Speedway Concert and the brutal murders by Charles Manson and his cohorts.

Extraordinary times of upheaval and change give birth to great art and heroic endeavors. The music of the Beatles and the poetry of Bob Dylan, the explosions in the art and fashion world, and the phenomenon of Woodstock, would culminate with a man walking on the moon.

Experiencing it all, we'd be both exhilarated and deeply wounded by what we saw.

My brother-in-law, Roddy, had returned from California for the holiday season of 1969. The year and the decade were coming to an end. To celebrate his return, and bid farewell to the 60's, we rented a room at The Plaza Hotel with the intention of throwing a big party.

My wife Angela, along with Roddy's closest friend, Bobby Perazzo, went to the hotel and posed as newlyweds. They were offered the Bridal Suite for one night at a cost of $100.

The night of the soiree, we packed a large suitcase with liquor and food. Filled with cold cuts, bread, cheese and Italian salami, we took the luggage and proceeded uptown to 59th Street and 5th Avenue. Upon arriving, Angela and Bobby signed in as the married couple. The Bell Hop came over to carry the valise into the elevator. Bobby wouldn't surrender it, and a tug-of-war ensued for several tense moments. It weighed considerably more than a bag filled with clothing should, and we didn't want to arouse any suspicions. In fact, the bag was so heavy, an outsider might believe there was a dead body in that trunk. The Bell Hop backed off when Bobby told him there was photography equipment inside, and he wanted to handle it himself. Being tall and strong was an advantage to Bobby in this situation. He managed to carry the suitcase with little visible effort.

We had planned for a small gathering. We were told we had to see the manager before going to our room. When he arrived, he apologized profusely, explaining how the Bridal Suite had inadvertently been rented out and was unavailable for the evening. However, he assured us we'd be pleased with its replacement.

We were brought up to the 5th floor, room 518. The large wooden Gothic door resembled a cathedral portal. There were two marble steps in front of the entrance and a metal plaque announcing the suite as The Senate State Room. When we entered, a collective gasp of exhilaration was let out. We had been given a private, five room, club. The lay out was breath taking. We took awhile to walk through the entire apartment savoring its grandeur. There were pictures of birds on many of the walls leading us to believe the suite belonged to The Audubon Society, or some similar organization.

The beveled bay windows in the huge living room faced 5th Avenue, looking out over the fountain in the plaza below. A large ornate marble fireplace graced the center of the room. Several leather couches and chairs were strategically placed, offering vantage points to view either the fireside within, or the Avenue with its shops and horse drawn carriages, without. A separate section off the dinning area contained a wet bar and entertainment complex.

This was beyond a luxury suite and we agreed the party was too small to befit the magnificent surroundings. We began calling other friends to join us in celebration. People began arriving with additional food and liquor. Jimmy Gilroy came with wine and cocaine. He had just graduated from bar tender school and put his knowledge to work behind the wet bar. The latest sensation was a mixture of various spirits with colours and cremes, called a Dirty Mother. These and other concoctions kept Jimmy busy. Cries of, "Hey, can you make another round of those Dirty Mother Fuckers?" continuously rang out. When Sharky arrived we all began sampling the grass and hashish. The mixture of food, liquor and drugs rivaled a bacchanalian feast.

From the small core group of myself and Angela, Roddy and Bobby, Kathy and Richie Lemole, the party mushroomed into a gathering of all our Greenwich Village family: Shark and his girlfriend Beth; Richie and Carla Palandrani; Cardo and Sherry Pecora; Nando and Mary Miguez; and Jimmy Gilroy and Annie Gonzalez. We partied all night. Recalling past adventures and discussing current circumstances, we enjoyed each other's company while simply getting wasted.

The evening became wilder and louder. Several of us found ourselves in an over-sized walk in closet. Drinking and consorting for some time, we exited wearing ladies bras and hats that we found, therein. Richie Palandrani had opened a window and was walking on an outside ledge. We convinced him to come back inside. If he wanted fresh air we'd go down for an excursion on the street.

It was a brutally cold December night. Richie, Cardo, Nando

and I, stoned out of our minds, and still wearing women's apparel, paraded out of the hotel. A walk around the neighborhood, we thought, would do us good. There were many things to see this time of year. The Christmas windows, St. Patrick's Cathedral, the tree in Rockefeller Center all were awaiting our scrutiny. A flurry of snow greeted us as we stumbled onto the sidewalk. We quickly realized we were in no condition to be outdoors. The traffic and cold proved to be too much for us. We hurriedly retreated back upstairs where the party continued into the wee hours of the morning.

When all the food, drinks and drugs were consumed we boarded the train going downtown to the Village, and home. We later learned Jimmy Gilroy and Annie Gonzalez slept over. Chocolates on the pillow and breakfast in bed were part of the original Bridal Suite rental. No one seemed to notice they weren't the couple who originally signed in as husband and wife. The shenanigans that occurred that night were comparable to a Marx Brother's movie.

Roddy's girlfriend from California, Diane, did not come east with him and missed attending the gathering. He invited a neighborhood girl, Linda, who we all met for the first time. Though quiet and reserved, everyone liked her. Fifteen years later, after his partnership with Diane was over, Roddy would marry Linda and have two sons.

The Bridal suite was available for Fernando and Mary's wedding. They kept ordering champagne all through the night. When presented with the bill, they were unable to pay it. The friends who had celebrated their wedding had to return and bail them out with the necessary cash.

Fernando and Mary and Ricardo and Sherry would become enamored with the Plaza. They would rent suites there over the next several years, for various occasions.

For us, that first night was the memorable one. Such an extravagant party in a private five room club was a fitting end to an era. The social upheaval left its mark. In contrast to the staid innocence of the 1950's, the revolutions of sex, drugs and rock & roll, in the following decade, would claim many victims. Bodies, souls and minds would be drawn to the allure of the free spirited 1960's and become lost within its excesses. A generation of friends, and strangers alike, would succumb to its indulgences.

I approached drugs as a tool to learn from, never using them to escape or solve any emotional or psychological problems. I wanted to have fun, experiment, and see first hand, what it was about. I was lucky to come out relatively unscarred, avoiding the burden of any life long addictions.

Aside from the experience, I walked away with these stories to tell. I knew enough not to go beyond a certain point. My constitution wasn't as strong as some of my friends. If I continued and did a fraction of the drugs they took over the coming years, I would not have survived.

I also realized at the close of the decade of the 1960's that the party was over. The two year period, 1968-1969, would bring changes to my life both personally and professionally. My vocation and avocation were competing forces that were approaching a head-on collision. Sustaining them both was becoming untenable. I was now married and a commitment to family and career was pressing. By year's end, one dream would see its end.

In September 1968, I decided to cut down my travel time and sought a transfer to Manhattan, the borough in which I lived. I was assigned to Frederick Douglas Junior High School 141 on 141st Street and Lennox Avenue in Harlem. It was another long, difficult year. Learning the ropes, adjusting to all the paper work and preparing lesson plans was time consuming.

Disciplining the students was another matter. I would often visit their gym class and engage the bigger and bothersome students in a wrestling match. I wanted them to know I could throw them around and handle them if I had to. It didn't help much.

The seasoned teachers counseled me to be patient. It takes about five years to become a good teacher. Routines and systems have to be established that vary for each individual. These, however, are discovered mostly by trial and error. No one can give you an exact formula for success. The only advice I received from my superiors when the class was acting up was to "keep them contained until the bell rings."

In the Spring term, I was updating my attendance books and noticed that several students had been absent for an unacceptable number of days. They lived on the block of the school and I decided to visit them during my lunch hour.

Upon entering the building, I was accosted by a man in a suit who introduced himself as Mr. Albano. He recognized me as a teacher from the neighborhood junior high school and asked what I was doing there. I told him the mission I was on. He explained that he was a "truant officer" or an Attendance Teacher and that visiting homes was his job.

He advised me of openings in the Bureau of Attendance and suggested I take the exam in the Spring for September hiring. I sat and past the test in early April. By August, I was issued the new license. Due to my curiosity, a new door had been opened that I did not know existed.

Two years of a difficult job had disillusioned me and I was ripe for change. I kept this in the back of my mind, not sure if I would alter my situation. Events at the end of this school year and the beginning of the next would hasten my decision.

In early June, a teacher was arrested while selling heroin out of his classroom. Buyers came in off the street to make their purchases. The story was covered by most of the local newspapers: *The Daily News*, *The New York Post* and *The Daily Mirror*. All the students were aware of the situation and were disturbed by it. It demoralized the staff.

I requested a transfer at the end of the school term and in September 1969 I found myself at Wadleigh Junior High School on 116th between Seventh and Eighth Avenues. I reported the Tuesday after Labor Day. The principal's used this time to interview prospective employees.

The place was overrun with children who had taken over the gymnasium and were rampaging throughout the building. Although students did not officially return until the following Monday, the school was already in chaos. I got a preview of what the coming year would be.

My resolve to go through that experience again dissolved when my eyes fell upon the teacher who had just been hired. Leaving the principal's office and being welcomed aboard was the man who was selling narcotics the previous school term. If the school was that desperate, it was worse than it appeared. I declined the interview and proceeded directly to the Board of Education headquarters at 65 Court Street, Brooklyn. For the next three days I sat outside the office of Eugene Cavanagh, Chief Attendance Officer of the Bureau of Attendance. At the end of the week, he came out and shook my hand, telling me I had a job as an Attendance Teacher in the East Side High School Division in Manhattan.

This new area of work would see me assigned to every school level over the course of my career. At one time or another, I would have the opportunity to work in elementary, junior high and high schools in all the boroughs of the city, except Staten Island.

The other part of my professional life, the group The Roman Numerals, was floundering. In the summer of 1969, on friendly terms, I would leave my band mates behind. They would continue to pursue the dream without me.

Entering graduate school in the Fall, in pursuit of a Master's Degree, I would take steps to secure my new license and position.

The Roman Numerals were not the only ones struggling. Dennis and I ran into our guitar teacher on the Upper West Side and were upset by what we saw. Lenny Pogan had been a mentor on the level of Irma Jurist. What Irma could do on the piano, Lenny could just about do on the guitar. When we first met him, he had been studying jazz for fifteen years and could play all styles of music. An accomplished guitarist, he played bass and banjo as well. In fact, he played the banjo lead on the hit record,

"Washington Square" in 1963. This group, The Village Stompers, was comprised of seven studio musicians. Lenny had achieved his playing ability despite the fact that one his fingers was mangled. He claimed he had severed the tip of the trigger finger on his left hand to avoid being drafted into the Vietnam War. This handicap kept him home, but in no way limited him. During the decade of the 60's, he was one of an elite group that were among the most sought after sidemen. He had to turn down recording sessions because of time constraints. He always wore a suit or tuxedo and was well groomed. This day, his hair was long and straggly, with his clothes unkempt. We asked how he was doing and he replied, "Not so well." Due to the enormous success of The Beatles, other groups followed suit and were providing their own instrumentation. This put many studio musicians out of work and Lenny, along with others, had hit upon hard times.

Just a few years earlier, he played featured rhythm guitar on our recording of "Matchstick in a Whirpool." He had been instrumental in polishing up the group's musicianship for those Columbia sessions. Through his tutelage, we gained a measure of respectability. Although we could not read or write music, we joined Local 802, in order to play alongside other union members.

On the B side, "The Come On," Lenny allowed me to play his D'Angelico "New Yorker." It was, and still remains, the best guitar I ever held. The action was light and smooth and the sound, with or without amplification, was full and clear. For jazz masters, who prefer an F hole, as opposed to a solid body instrument, these guitars were comparable to Stradavari.

Lenny, in need of quick cash, offered to sell me his beloved baby for $3,000. By the time John D'Angelico died in the 1980's, he had hand crafted a finite number of instruments. As the decades passed their value has soared. Today, depending on the year and model, some of his guitars approach $100,000 in resale.

We were disheartened by Lenny's downfall. I would have been happy to purchase the New Yorker. However, I had my own obligations and could not squander what amounted to nearly a half-year's salary on such a luxury.

Work, career, graduate school, the birth of my son, Aubrey, in 1972, and his brother, Arden, fourteen months later, gave new direction and purpose to my life. My time living in the Village was coming to an end.

For various reasons we decided to move out of the city. Perhaps we simply wanted something different for our children than what we had known. A safer environment, offering quality schools and the general prospect of a better life led us to New Jersey. There, we began a new period in our lives. We knew in our hearts what we left behind would always be with us.

Epilogue

Living had noticeably changed during the twenty-five year period from my birth in 1945 to the close of the decade in 1969.

The mobility afforded by the automobile now separated families by great distances. Initially, this affluence brought access to the suburbs of the metropolis. As jobs were lost to other parts of the country, city dwellers left with them. Due to this trend, and for reasons of personal choice, I have family living in the states of Arizona, California, North and South Carolina, Florida, Maryland, Michigan, Nevada, New Jersey, Tennessee, Texas, Virginia and Washington.

Once, we all gathered for Sunday dinner at my grandmother's on Bleecker Street across from Our Lady of Pompeii Church and School. Those were the happiest times. All my cousins together, with my aunts and grandma preparing, cooking and eating an elaborate, yet simple, meal. Everyone talked about the trials and tribulations in their current lives, and their hopes and aspirations for the future.

The now defunct art of making a meal from scratch was common practice then, and something to behold. My grandmother would make the dough from flour, water, yeast and eggs. It would sit for a long time waiting to rise. On the large kitchen table she'd roll it flat with a long wooden pin. When it was the right thickness the women would transfer the pasta to a bed covered with a white sheet. This would continue until the entire sheet was filled.

The next step was to make the ricotta filling for the ravioli. The secret was adding just the right amount of salt, pepper, nutmeg and/or cinnamon, for a delicious cheese center.

Although my Uncle Pro was an excellent cook, learning from his father the chef, this meal belonged to grandma, with her daughters assisting. The rest of us, my cousins Joan and Joseph, Yolanda, Kathy and Jacki, along with my sister Carole and I, anxiously anticipated the meal to follow.

Things moved slowly and it took patience to produce such a feast. Provided we washed our hands first, grandma would allow all the children to put their finger in a bowl filled with ricotta, to sample her creation. Meanwhile, the gravy was cooking with plenty of meatballs and sausage.

The meal was topped off with wonderful desserts. Fresh *cannoli* from the pastry shops downstairs, and other home made confections, completed the meal. The round honey glazed *struffole*, covered with sprinkles, and the feathery layered *sfogliatelle*, were two special treats. The St. Joseph's cruller was a seasonal pastry enjoyed by all during the period of the saint's feast day, March 19th.

Invariably, an aunt dressed in the ever present house coat would place her hands across her voluminous breasts, and inquire, "Black or brown?" This, to a trained observer, meant the choice of espresso or American coffee.

These gatherings occurred sporadically during my youth and adolescence. The last child of that generation, Theresa, would be born to join us in our family repast. However, as my cousins and I approached adulthood, other interests separated us.

The passing of the ritual of the entire family gathering for Sunday dinner, was a loss for us all.

Times changed and so had the Village. Gone were the days when people hung out the windows and sat on the fire escapes. No longer to be seen were the street musicians. These traveling troubadours, who came on the scene mainly in summer, would serenade the populace with standards or the latest popular tunes. Throwing down change, which was collected in a hat, prompted a song in your dedication.

Another staple that became dispensable was the iceman. Refrigerators, along with television, had taken over. Radio lost some of its appeal while the icebox became a dinosaur.

As a young child I have faded memories of some buildings still using dumb-waiters. These were small hand operated elevators that ran through the apartments. By pulling a set of chains, food, trash and other items were transported from one floor to another, giving tenants access to family members or neighbors living above or below. Over time these devices were sealed over and eventually vanished from use.

Telephones were rapidly advancing. The round phones with rotary dials gave way to heavy desk models. These evolved into wall units with extension cords that still utilized a finger dial. The old exchanges, Adirondack (AD), Bigelow (BI), Murray Hill (MH), Oregon (OR), Spring (SP), Trafalgar (TR), and Watson (WA), were no longer in use. More than half a century later, I still recall my first telephone number on Jones Street—CH-2-0907. The exchange was Chelsea.

The people who traveled around in utility trucks to shine pots and pans, and sharpen knives and other tools, were gone. The Fuller Brush Man, The Good Humor Truck and G.I. Joe's hot dog stands, all had seen their day. Avon calling, had its ups and downs, but managed to survive.

One of the biggest cultural changes was the loss of the pushcarts that lined Bleecker Street. They lasted several generations. The Italians sold fruits, vegetables and other produce from these stands, stretching from Carmine Street to 7th Avenue South.

The loss of the roof, as a wondrous escape, was the final blow. Here was a magical place, an oasis that calmed the stress of urban life. A place to be alone, and put aside the world and its burdens. A place to get fresh air and relax. At night, a chance to gaze upon the stars in reverie.

Another feature of the roofs were the multitude of pigeon coops adorning them. Poor people, who couldn't afford the racetrack, or other expensive indulgences, used this outlet for sport and entertainment.

When you couldn't get to the seashore, there was always the poor man's alternative, "Tar Beach." My mother and sister spent countless hours up there, lying on a blanket and basking to a golden bronze.

Many of the traditions we embraced growing up in Greenwich Village are no longer practiced. Through the ebb and flow that is characteristic of a constantly changing city, many things tend to slip away. Despite all the changes, something very powerful always draws me back.

In the late 1980's, I was living in the Bronx. My Uncle Pro and Aunt Marie were still residing in their house in Flushing, Queens. I offered to take them out to dinner. Pro had to check his calendar before presenting a satisfactory date. After considering who died, or went to the hospital, or suffered a variety of traumas, he was left with just a handful to choose from. On these days, my uncle could go out and enjoy himself without feeling any guilt.

As an aide to my memory, I find myself marking my calendar by denoting birthdays and deaths of family members and friends. By the nature of things each year there are additions. I do not limit myself from celebrating on any particular day, but I do, in some way, recognize the passing of events that occurred on individual dates. The older I become, the more I can empathize with my uncle's feelings.

I decided to take them to Zinno's Jazz Club and Restaurant on 13th Street, in the Village. It was owned and operated by my old friend, Bobby Perazzo. Before dinner we took a walk around the neighborhood. Pro and Marie were delighted to see things they remembered, yet acutely aware of the many changes that took place since they grew up there in the 1920's and 30's. When passing the Pompeii Church and School, my uncle paused to look up at the third floor apartment at 243 Bleecker Street. He stood there transfixed. After sating his desire, he turned to me and said, "I can still see my mother smiling at the window."

Is that what calls me back? The hope of seeing someone from my past. A chance to glimpse an old friend turning the corner, especially those who are gone. To see Donald, Gerard and Danny, once again, when we were young, when the Village belonged to us, and we were free from the burdens and responsibility life would later bestow.

Perhaps its appeal lies in a simpler life remembered. Or the memory of a life rich in appeal. Either way, you can sometimes find me at Richie and Carla Palandrani's, Greenwich Village Bistro, having a meal and a drink. Maybe I'll see you there one day. We can have a beer or a glass of wine and reminisce about the old neighborhood. In that process I can think of the Village as I remember it. And I can remember the Village when it was mine.

Alfred and Carole Canecchia at the
Greenwich Settlement House, Christmas 1948.

Sixth Avenue, Northwest from West 8th Street and Greenwich Avenue (1938)

Women's House of Detention

Dennis (Shark) Guglielmo. Cosmic observer. Entrepreneur. Oenophile.

The Feast of St. Anthony of Padua on Sullivan Street.

Vincent (Jimmy) Gambino.
The Bambino who led a rough and tumble life.

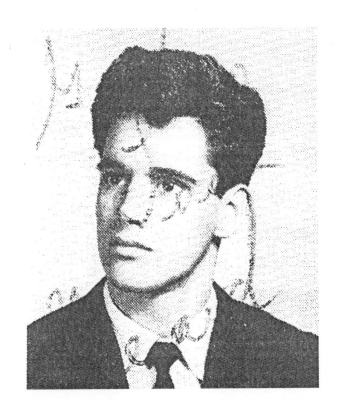

Gerard Gabriel Madison

Robert (Ziggy) Andriani. The Pied Piper. King Lonely,
The Blue, from an oil rendition by Robert Villanti.

Irma Jurist. Singer, pianist, composer.

Lucien Barnes IV standing in the doorway of his guitar shop on
Carmine Street with Dennis Genovese, 1965.

The Roman Numerals, promotional photo for the release of
"Matchstick in a Whirlpool," on Columbia Records 1967.
Front row from left to right: Alfred Canecchia, Daniel Marsicovetere,
Dennis Genovese. In rear with guitar, John Marsicovetere.
Personal Management: Elaine Sorel, 129 West 56th Street,
New York, NY 10019.

The Roman Numerals performing at The Bitter End Café, 1966.

Acknowledgements

The following have helped me to remember: Bruno Abate, Sergio Bosi, Thomas Bruno, Angela DiStefano Canecchia, Joseph Canecchia, Edward Colaci, Louis Ferrarese, Dennis Genovese, Dominick Joseph Genovese, Jr., James Gilroy, Dennis Guglielmo, Peter Guglielmo, William & Jean Hartnett, Rocco Iacovone, Lillian Lamarsch Intemann, Carole Canecchia Lazarus, Robert Leake, Kathleen Pope & Richard Lemole, Yolanda Volpe & Richard Lorraine, Mary Madison, John Marsicovetere, Salvatore Mazzarella, Sandra Briand Merino, David Noferi, Richard & Carla Lewis Palandrani, Ricardo & Sharon Pecora, Robert Perazzo, Louise Perazzo, Rita Platt, Kathleen Quinto, Jacki Quinto Spagna, Joseph Turchiano, Patrick Vallance and Robert Villanti.

Thanks to the following individuals for editing and technical assistance: Roberta Campli Canecchia, Donna Dale, Charles Garvey, David Grosz, Devorah Grosz, Diane Kwitnicki, Eileen McSweeney, Hedy Minerbo, and Judith Veder Scheinbach.

Special thanks to Alvin Goldsmith and Gary Lazarus for many hours of transferring these stories onto the computer and printing them up.

And to my wife, Roberta, for hours of proof reading, encouragement and help with the English language. Her patience in living without a dining table for extended periods of time is appreciated.

Appendix A

Village Nicknames

Albie Goof

Anita Chinkaweena

Anthony Bags

Anthony Bread

Baby Brown

Bambino

Batman

B-Bomb

Beak (Johnny,
     Philly)

Benny Eggs

Bibs

Biddy

Big D

Bing

Bird

Blacky

Blindy Joey

Bobby Rock

Boobie

Boots

Bosco

Brother

Brother Fat

Butch

Butchie

Cappy

Charley Baa—Baa

Charley Sauseech

Cheech

Chico

Chin

C.I. (Crime Inc.)

Cigarette Annie

Cochise

Cockeyed Joey

Coney Island Rose

Cookie

Corky

Crazy Carlo

Crazy Louie

Crazy Raymond

Crazy Rosie

Crazy Vinny

Danny Bull

Dapper Dan

Dennis Pimple Ass

Dirty Draws

Dist

Dom Black

Dom Joe

Dom the Sailor

Doody

Fat Anna

Fat Joe

Fatman

Fats

Fits

Fritzy

Gaga

Gagoots

Gazut

Gene Fa-Ta-Boom

G.I. Joe

Goo-Goo

Gumaah

Happy

Harry the Head

Helen the Mick

I Don't Know

Jake Spook

Jimmy Blue

Jimmy Spade

Joe Action

Joey Head

Johnny Boy

Johnny Bull

John-John

JO JO Clams

Jumbo

Jumbo Wood

Junior

Lenny Cooch

Lenny Goon

Leo(n) Vitamins

Little Joe

Little Rich

Louie the Lug

Luck n Lay

Marie Three
     Minutes

Mikie Black
     (Beulah)

Mikie G

Mikie Jap

Min

Modie

Moe-Moe

Moochy

Mouse (Franky,
Johnny, Danny)

Nickles

Patsy Geesh

Pecos Bill

Peter Shark

Peetie Chink

Peetie Pecker

Peetie the Tramp

Polly

Poochie

Professor (Pro)

Pussy

Rags

Ralphie Beast

Richie Dit

Richie Fart (Fot)

Robert Red

Rocky

Russian Ronnie

Sallie Hat

Sallie Pebbles

Scratch

Shark (Sharky)

Shorty

Sister

Skinny

Skippy

Slave Girl Moola

Smelly

Snowball

Sonny

Sonny Hap

Sputzie

Stilts

Superman

The Cut

The Ham

Tilly

Ting-a-Ling

Tiny

Tommy Besh

Tommy Light Bulb

Tommy Pie (Pie
     Face)

Tommy Seven

Tommy the Priest

Tom-Tom

Tony Botts

Tony the Bug

Vinny Deaf &
     Dumb

Vinny Mustache

Vinny Sauseech

Vinny the Jap

Wee (Weetsie)

Ziggy

Zippy

Appendix B

Gentrification of the Village

**GREENWICH
VILLAGE $685,000**

15 Jones St.
One-bedroom, two-bath
prewar duplex co-op,
850 square feet, with
child's room, renovated
kitchen and bath,
exposed brick, skylight,
N/W exposures and
private terrace.
Maintenance $1,262.
Asking price $685,000,
on market one day.
*(Brokers: Ed Blankenship and
Nan Schiff, Douglas Elliman)*

Appendix C

HARD TO GET LOVE

(Christmas 1967)

Can you see the bullets fly
As the Arabs fell?
Can you hear the children
Crying out in Israel?
It's not hard to see
There's no love for free
Was this ever really a land,
A holy land?

And do they have a setting sun
In far off Vietnam?
Did we really have a war
With our friends in Japan?
Who can understand?
You need a war to shake a hand
Was there ever really a town
Called Bethlehem?

Where has love gone?
Where has love gone?
Where has love gone?
Where has love gone?

Hard to get love, hard to get love
Hard to get love, hard to get love
Hard to get love, hard to get love
Hard to get love, It's so hard to get love

We can send a ship through space
To explore a foreign land
Yet the greatest distance
Still lies from man to man
Will we ever see
We need love to set us free?
Then we'll have a world
Of harmony.

Glory be, to the newborn king!

Composed by:
John Marsicovetere
Arranged and Sung by:
The Roman Numerals

BVG